Finding Our Way *Home*

Three Dynamics of Christian Recovery

Charles Determan Sr.

WESTBOW
PRESS®
A DIVISION OF THOMAS NELSON
& ZONDERVAN

Scriptures taken from the Holy Bible, New International Version®, NIV®.
Copyright © 1973, 1978, 1984, 2011 by Biblica, Inc.™ Used by permission
of Zondervan. All rights reserved worldwide. www.zondervan.com The
"NIV" and "New International Version" are trademarks registered in
the United States Patent and Trademark Office by Biblica, Inc.

WestBow Press books may be ordered through booksellers or by contacting:

WestBow Press
A Division of Thomas Nelson & Zondervan
1663 Liberty Drive
Bloomington, IN 47403
www.westbowpress.com
1 (866) 928-1240

ISBN: 978-1-9736-3513-0 (sc)
ISBN: 978-1-9736-3514-7 (hc)
ISBN: 978-1-9736-3512-3 (e)

Library of Congress Control Number: 2018908817

Print information available on the last page.

WestBow Press rev. date: 08/06/2018

Contents

Dedication

Fr. Ken Smits, pastor Dave Katsma and my wife Jennie without whose inspiration, guidance and support this book would not have been possible.

Preface

As I reflected on my reasons for wanting to write this book I have often been haunted by a question, "What do I have to say that has not been already said about Recovery?" My answer is that my experience in recovery has allowed me to recognize how difficult the process of recovery has been and is becoming especially for those who sense a connection with a power greater than themselves but who are intimidated by a world which seems to have jettisoned God long ago. It is important to admit that this intimidation has roots because of certain shifts that have occurred in the background of belief as our global society has moved forward into modernity. As far as this book goes I have no interest in delving into the complex theories surrounding the rise of secularity but I do want to talk about that which is present in spite of it. There is a presence (*a dynamic living presence*) that always militates against the human tendency to find meaning that rests in the mind alone.

We must also admit; although, that reason is an amazing tool which helps to make the world an efficient and productive place but it also can at times be found wanting. This whole situation is played out as one scientist wars against another, as one hypothesis is thrown upon the rocky shore of invalid data and another is championed as the best possible conclusion. An example of this would be the mammoth pharmaceutical world in which drugs (that claim to cure whatever) come and go and there is one for every occasion and every ill. It seems that every new drug is accompanied by a marketing plan to ensure its success, in terms of sales and profit, regardless of its success in the real world. My question is, What does this "productivity and profit at any cost attitude" do to the mind of the common man? My answer is, He (she) doesn't just become cynical, he also becomes callous, egocentric and self centered. He becomes conditioned by society, the automaton who sets out to accomplish the task of wrenching a tolerable existence from a hostile world. The questions continue on…*ad infinitum.* How do we make the choice of faith valid? How is it that so many seem to leave a small piece of their self open to religious notions? How is it that there is such a huge gap between having religious notions and living a religious life? And as we try to answer these questions we see that the same problem that science faces is also faced by religion whenever it is treated as that which is scientific, that which can be dissected and explained, it becomes extremely complex and this complexity does more to bury the answers than to bring them to life.

> *"I keep remembering Kierkegaard's gripe with Hegel – that he'd (Hegel) figured out everything, with all the theorizing he did about history and time and ideas and their impact on one another; but he left out one thing, how it goes for people from one day to another: the history of someone getting through an ordinary day"* (Richard Coles, *A Secular Mind*)

It is my hope that this book is not seen as some sort of attempt to answer philosophical questions but rather as just another hand in recovery that is reaching out to help an ordinary man or woman get through an ordinary day by becoming reacquainted with the living dynamic presence of God. This process is what I have come to see as a valid alternative to wrenching a tolerable existence out of a hostile world.

Introduction

Those who are fortunate enough to experience recovery generally do not work the 12 steps with any kind of strictness or discipline. More often than not the philosophy behind the steps and the deeper ideas contained within are absorbed (*one becomes porous to the Spirit*) over time as a person learns to live and value a new way of life. The beginner may be strongly encouraged to become familiar with the steps and accept 1, 2 and 3 and get on with preparing a fourth step but after the initial groundwork is done the person in recovery is necessarily left to work out their own journey as they *"seek through prayer and meditation to improve their relationship with God as they understand him."*[i] Now, there are 12 step meetings etc…where people can review the importance of the steps but my overall point would be that they are usually not walking around asking themselves, "OK, what step am I on today and what do I need to be doing to keep myself on track to make it to the next step". What I have noticed is that people are actively trying to "find their way" and that their attention to the steps waxes and wanes as their daily life plays out, especially as the years pass in recovery. And it is this "waxing and waning" that I believe is governed by three dynamics that are at work throughout a person's life in recovery. Each one of these dynamics presents itself as a kind

---

[i] Alcoholics Anonymous, 3rd edition, AA World Services Inc, New York, p59

of continuum where we all find ourselves to be in different positions at different times. It is the awareness of these working dynamics (their aliveness) that can give an individual a frame from which to begin to see the realistic possibility of having a true heartfelt relationship with a power greater than them self. These dynamics are distance vs closeness, stagnation vs process and complexity vs simplicity. I have chosen to pair each of these dynamics with a scripture verse from the book of Romans. Paul has a way of talking about the tension of the Christian life which in my opinion is directly applicable to the dynamic conflict that is experienced by one who is in recovery (*and even by many who are not*). Today the recovery movement can be looked upon as encapsulating many different forms of recovery ranging from drug and alcohol abuse to overeating and codependency and many other problems that present a person with a challenging circumstance from which to recover even including those who struggle with religion (recovering Christians). Within this expanse is a definite group of individuals that have become "disenchanted" with organized religion of any sort. This disenchantment has been written about at great length by a number of authors (Charles Taylor, Marcel Gauchet, Lillian Daniel…) and the general conclusion seems to be that organized religion no longer holds the same power of attraction that it once did. This loss of attraction in large part is attributed at least in some ways to the advance of science as it ushered in the industrial revolution. This revolution was accompanied by a corresponding reduction in the way people viewed their dependence on the role of the church in their life. In other words they began to no longer stand in absolute fear about things like angels and demons and the judgment of God because they saw the impact that science was having in terms of increasing production as well as, especially in modernity, people's health and life expectancy. The way in which this progression has taken place can be forever examined through the lens of history but what has become crystal clear through the lens of everyday life is that there is an ever growing population of people that can (and perhaps should) be seen as being in recovery from organized religion. To treat this condition of disenchantment as if it is not debilitating, as if it does not affect the quality of our lives, as if it is not a condition that predisposes one towards developing more serious problems including addiction is in my mind a serious mistake. As human beings we all thirst for meaning and one of the best ways to quench this thirst is to examine whether or not it is possible for an individual to grasp some sort of understanding of the mystery and miracle of life. Often such an understanding can be the first step in seeing organized religion in the light of community as opposed to the light of judgment. It is my hope and prayer that the following presentation of recovery dynamics will not only be useful to anyone struggling with formal recovery issues but also as a voice which is saying, "I hear you", to all those who don't know how to interact with a power greater than themselves but who still want so much to see and feel how such a thing is possible even in today's complex and modern world.

In addition I would like to make clear that for a long period in my life I was a religious skeptic, I believed that reason itself was calling far too much into question as far as organized religion went...yet there was a part of myself that was always open to listening to what others had to say about religion and God. If you have this openness then you have the same invitation to love yourself, God and others that was given to me and I would like to encourage you to press on by accepting how you can forever learn more about your relation to God.

Dynamic One – Distance vs Closeness

"And men go abroad to admire the heights of mountains, the mighty waves of the sea, the broad tides of rivers, the compass of the ocean, and the circuits of the stars, yet pass over the mystery of themselves without a thought." Augustine of Hippo, *Confessions.*

The first and what I see as the most popular barrier to recovery is when a person experiences the distance of God as opposed to His closeness. An image quickly comes to mind of a lone individual standing in some sort of great expanse, a desert or endless dark space where they find them self unconnected to something that they somehow miss. It is interesting to note that in order to miss something we must have in some way known it before in a meaningful way. For me this is the kind of reflection that requires a sort of sinking into oneself or an exploration of our inner world. It is an exploration because it involves an inward turn, no longer are we looking for something that we can hold in our hand but rather something that is already held in our heart. The subjective or abstract nature of this type of reflection is often used as a reason for its avoidance but if we want to succeed in recovery it is a necessity. If we lack the desire to see an accurate and honest reflection of who we are our progress in recovery will be severely limited. Sometimes making a beginning is like laying the first stone of a pathway but often there just doesn't seem to be any stones available. The construction of one's path can begin with an admission that we have an emotional side and that this emotional side stands in addition to or as a complement to our reason. This admission can usher in or invite the realization that we are more than a one dimensional thinking being, that we have a depth to our nature that represents something worth exploring. We can begin to see that there is some type of underlying current within us all (which science confirms), some call it emotion, some call it the collective unconscious, some call it the presence of love. The point is that the acknowledgement that we have this inner dimension can be one of the most important stones that we lay on the pathway of recovery. But often we insist on focusing on our self in our *"aloneness"* (in the great dark expanse of distance). From this position of aloneness we lack the ability or the desire to explore the depth of our life. In this locked or frozen perspective we have no choice but to define our self only by what we do or accomplish (*on the surface of things*) and this can be done at the expense of a connection with something greater than our self.

> *"The real spiritual guide is the one who, instead of advising us what to do or to whom to go, offers us a chance to stay alone and take the risk of entering into our own experience. He makes us see that pouring little bits of water on our dry land does not help, but that we will find a living well if we reach deep enough under the surface of our complaints."*[1] (Henri Nouwen, *Reaching Out*)

If we succeed in reconnecting with this power (that is greater than our self) we also reconnect with our self at a much deeper level, we find that we not only have value because of what we do but also because we are a human being, and as such made in the image of God. But this whole notion of sinking into oneself can be problematic especially when our daily lives are spent on the surface of things, getting done what needs to get done, it is difficult finding time to sink within, it is difficult finding understanding, it is difficult finding deep and lasting meaning. One of the things that I have found helpful is to use an overall metaphor to reflect on the structure of our inner world. The metaphor that I would like to suggest is to think of our inner world as a cosmos or miniature universe.[ii] We are all aware that we live in a planetary cosmos/ universe and that what gives our cosmos order and balance is the way in which planets orbit a central sun. I would like to invite us all to shift our perspective so that we are no longer gazing outward at the marvelous way in which our planetary system is held in balance but rather are gazing inward so that we also can become aware of the necessary balance that should and can be maintained within our inner world or cosmos as well.

We live in a technologically advanced world which is capable of producing incredible "special effects" especially in relation to the world of cinema. It is easy to look at all of these creations and be aware that even though they amaze our eyes and can manipulate our emotion they also were created by another human being. As a result when the time comes that we are asked to use our imagination to examine our inner world we may tend to stumble or fumble about as if we have entered a place for the very first time. In our daily life all of the special effects are provided for us and they are amazing because other people have the technology and equipment to produce them. So if we are going to take the reins of our own imagination it can be beneficial to start off slow. We can begin by focusing on our sense of awareness...we are conscious of

---

[ii] Please see chapter 7 for further explanation of the history of this concept.

the world around us and this awareness is part of us. Although our consciousness is generally associated with the organ of the brain we also know that the brain needs input from the senses and that the body and brain together are used to produce consciousness. But this consciousness does not seem to have a physical form but yet is undeniably real. It is this formlessness that gives our consciousness the ability to investigate our inner world.

All scientific investigation is first inspired by an active imagination which seeks to confirm or deny an intuition. Let us remember that taking a look at our inner world is not about checking ourselves into to some sort of clinic where we can have some 3–D imagery done of our physical body. What we are after here is a self reflective examination of our consciousness that is hopefully inspired by a part of us that has always been aware of or deeply sensed that there is something within us that is worth our attention and that this something leaves all our advanced technology severely wanting. Our consciousness contains our current understanding of ourselves and the world in which we live. This understanding is sometimes taken for granted and in no way associated with something that should be questioned or looked upon as something that is growing and evolving or in a state of becoming what it was always meant to be. So as we begin to make a serious inward turn there is often a natural tendency to want to know the makeup of our most basic parts (*to skip ahead and get the one answer we are really after!*) what it is that gives us life and therefore makes us who we are. Using our consciousness, as well as information we can glean from science, we can begin to analyze the structure of our physical bodies and quickly take ourselves apart (metaphorically) to the point at which we are confronted with the smallest structures that makeup our bodies. We are held together by molecules, tiny structures that somehow create invisible bonds. Within these structures are protons and electrons rotating about a nucleus which in a gravity defying act floats in the center of each and every molecule. If we could pass through a molecule…if we could shrink ourselves down and come to rest on an electron I wonder if we would experience a kind of sunset as we would undoubtedly witness how other particles rotating around us would block a clear line of sight to our nucleus. I wonder how different this scene would be if our molecule was positioned in back of an eye where light was somehow being captured and focused or resting in a section of the brain that was somehow glowing because of a chemical reaction from the rise and fall of emotion.

Depending on our perspective it is possible to see whole other universes within our own universe. It is this kind of seeing which can begin to lay the groundwork for not only witnessing the mystery and miracle of life but also encourage a much more fundamental observation. The beauty, mystery and wonder of our inner and outer lives have never been explained away by reason but exist in the same proportion that it always has and as a result it literally fills the world. It is clear that at some point we will all confront the mystery and miracle of life, the challenge that I extend is to see the value of having this confrontation today. If we do entertain this notion we cannot avoid looking at our self in relation to the rest of the world

> *Do not be conformed to the patterns of this world but*
> *be transformed by the renewing of your mind.* Rom
> 12:2

When I read this verse I immediately think, what are some of the patterns of this world? Many people who are in recovery believe in God but their relationship is one of distance because God is not seen as helpful or something that should be helpful with the nuts and bolts of daily life (the surface of things). God is consciously positioned on an outer orbit, yes he is watching, yes we can look up and experience a sense of awe, especially around the holidays but the individual is the engine that runs daily life. God is regulated to an outer orbit because work, family, bill paying and keeping up with the Joneses or meeting society's expectations require the steadfast attention of our daily lives. The problem is that a distant God can easily become a God who is focused on only in times of need and on the opposite end of this spectrum this perception can also have the affect of leading to a god of our own creation whom we invest with qualities that we determine depending on what makes sense to us at any given time (privatized spirituality).

This type of privatized spirituality seems to be very popular in our modern world.

> *"The "nones," a category that includes people who self-identify as atheists or agnostics, as well as those who say their religion is "nothing in particular," now make up 23% of U.S. adults, up from 16% in 2007. But there is more to the story. To begin with, this group is not uniformly nonreligious. Most of them say they believe in God, and about a third say religion is at least somewhat important in their lives."* (Pew Research Center, Religious "Nones" becoming more secular, Micheal Lipka 2015)

My belief is that this popularity is due to the fact that private self created spirituality requires very little from the busy, distracted and sometimes indifferent individual or it in other words comes with no real cost.

> *"No sacrifice which a lover would make for his beloved is too great for us to make for our enemy."* (Dietrich Bonhoeffer, *The Cost of Discipleship*)

True spirituality is always costly, it always requires an examination of self which can often lead to a type of death as the old self is transformed into the new self. This situation; although, can be quite confusing to the beginner who has an interest in leading a spiritual life. What seems important and what is often taught is that a personal heartfelt relationship with God is what spirituality is all about. So if the personal relationship is what it is all about than why are people being criticized for following their own path in forming such a relationship? The answer to this question is found by realizing that if as an individual we have truly found the love of God we cannot help but at some point want to share this love with others in community. It is within such a loving community or church that an exchange of ideas and learning can take place to enrich and verify that what we see as a valid relationship with God is indeed a valid representation and not something that we have unconsciously constructed to our own benefit. Often scripture can be used to verify and enhance this growing relationship with God. Many people would perhaps argue against the necessity of having one's personal relationship with God verified by one's faith community proclaiming that there are many non religious (or many "nones") that have done great things for the world in which they live and to this I would have to agree. The main point that I would want to make is that in as much as we can rightly see ourselves as individual and unique expressions of life when it comes to our conception of our relationship to God it is in some ways always shrouded in mystery, this mystery deserves not only our own individual investigation but also the holding up of our own investigation to the light of history. We need to humbly hold our conception of our relation to God because when it comes to how to understand God there are no geniuses, we should be always ready to see our relation to God change or grow. It is in the atmosphere of a faith community that we can give the best expression to the mystery that is God. It is not about some sort of constant debate or the mathematician standing before the dry erase board constantly grinding out another equation but rather it is about sensing and coming to know the presence of God in an atmosphere of love.

One of the most significant ways to work against privatized spirituality is to promote the common sense realization that positioning God on the outer orbit of our lives completely removes him from "the center" (of our lives) and if God is not the center of our lives than we have become the center about which everything revolves and if we are the center we can have only one champion and that champion becomes our self.

This celebration of self (ego) is another pattern of this world. As individuals of the material world we are encouraged to believe in ourselves, to dream big, to never give up and to try ever harder to succeed. There is nothing at all wrong with dreaming big and trying ever harder to succeed but when and if we determine our success solely by characteristics that society defines we set ourselves up for emotional upheaval or failure because when we encounter hardship or depression we end up with a distant God whom we have no idea how to relate to in a personal and heartfelt way. When we learn to see the place of God at the center of our inner cosmos we can also learn that in addition to believing in the God given value and dignity of our self we can also experience faith and it is this gift of faith that begins the renewing of our mind. Here, we can begin to see the pathway taking shape, that in as much as laying the first stone seemed to be an arduous task we now begin to see that we were never truly alone and with God's grace we begin to witness the transformation of our inner universe.

If and when the patterns of this world begin to lose their gravitational pull we also can begin to see how a transcendent (outer) God can also be an immanent (inner) God. In scripture we are told that Christ had to die so that the advocate (Spirit) could come. (John 16). If we accept the notion that the Holy Spirit is the third person of the Trinity (1 Cor 8:6) and that each person of the trinity is connected by the ongoing movement or outpouring of love (John 17: 20-26), one resulting conclusion can be that the presence of the Spirit within us represents an immanent God who has the ability of influence in our life through grace and love. But as we execute the patterns of this world we create or attach value to things or perceptions (which can become the rotating planets of our inner universe) and the more and more we learn to depend on the affirmation that comes from acquiring these things and perceptions the more we insist on creating our own world and especially our own inner world.

There are not many of us who have been given the creative talent and potential of an artist. We do; although, create our own ideas and conceptions especially as we are trying to conform to the patterns of our world. As we are busy exercising this creative ability it is as if we are an "idea" artist and we are sitting at some sort of bench or station and have been given some sort of media or clay which we mold into thought. The question is where does our inspiration come from? Does it come from the God who is within and without or from that which is appreciated and valued by the material world? It is as if we somehow forget that in as much as our divine center exerts a gravitational pull it also gives off rays of light in the form of inspiration and influence. In the last analysis it seems obvious to me that it is, in some limited ways, necessary to conform to some of the patterns of this world so that we can achieve a certain level of success that allows us to survive in a life that is without overwhelming pain and suffering. But if we can keep God close and keep ourselves humble (avoid the celebration of self) we may be able to prevent the forming of some kind of barrier between ourselves and God. The more we allow our distance from God to stand and go unchecked it is as if we begin to seal off or sequester

God into some sort of protected room or hidden space and as a result there is a part of us that begins to grow callous, God is present but not needed. We are now no longer porous to the Spirit.

It is also interesting to note that even when a person does remain porous to the Spirit he or she can often act on the mistaken impression that they must transcend this world. This is where the incarnation of Christ teaches us a valuable lesson. Christ became human to show us how to be fully human, to show us the sacredness of humanity.

> *"For we do not have a high priest that is unable to empathize with our weaknesses, but we have one that has been tempted in every way, just as we are – yet he did not sin."* Heb 4:15

Our task therefore is not to shake off the patterns of this world and somehow float above it, to ignore it, to disparage it, to give up on it, but rather "to see" how the patterns of this world prevent us from being truly human and experiencing the true healing freedom that human fullness can bring.

Those that see God as an arbitrary and unloving God, (who is positioned on an outer orbit) do so as a result of seeing God as separate from us…purely transcendent.

> *"They naturally pray for the good things they want and relief from the bad things we don't want. And usually it doesn't work. We don't get all we want, and we get too much of what we don't want. Logically then, that transcendent, omnipotent, and separate God seems arbitrary at best and unloving at worst."*[2]

An alternative view would be that the power of God may not extend to making God invulnerable.

*"Most contemplatives see God as being wounded when
and as we are wounded, sharing our sufferings as well
as our joys. There is a sense that the Holy One has been
surrendered to us in love, and **needs** us to love, to be
loved by and to manifest God's love in the world."*[3]

I have always found this outlook to be much more helpful and honest as it gives voice to a God who is not distant but rather is standing beside us in our grief, weeping with us...helping us to heal.

Closeness is born and nurtured in Prayer

The following is a short study of John 17:21-23, there is no mention of a "tear" falling from the face of Christ in the verses them self, it is just a feeling that I came away with after reflecting on the anguish and love of Christ's prayer for us. It is important that when we attempt to sink within ourselves in order to seek out and find balance (an inner cosmos at rest) that we realize that the thought process in which we are now dwelling marks a great beginning in that we are wading into the waters of meditation and prayer. Our initial attempts to pray or spend time in quiet meditation (as we reflect on things that have gone wrong as well as things that have gone right in our life) will always pale in comparison to the prayer of Christ but one must always remember, *"that the quality of prayer is never determined by one's abilities, but rather by the graced willingness to depend upon the Lord and to allow the Spirit to pray within oneself as It will."*[4]

*That all of them may be one, Father, just as you are
in me and I am in you. May they also be in us so that
the world may believe that you have sent me. (vs. 21)*

In order for the world to believe they must see and then will be able to know the presence…We ask our self, do people see the presence in us or do they see downcast souls? Our heaviness cannot be compared with His. Yes, we fall short, we always will. There most certainly is a gravitational pull…there are always things competing for the center. He must not be displaced. We must keep being drawn to the shape of things. Three overlapping circles (God, Jesus, us) with an intersecting space. There is a part we hold in common, this being our relation to God (and Jesus) and His relation to us.

I have given them the glory that you gave me, that they may be one as we are one (vs. 22)

We have been enabled to seek unity with one another as believers. Jesus has given us the indwelling presence of God and in so doing allows all believers to share in the same sense of unity that he shares with the Father.

> *I in them and you in me – so that they may be brought to complete unity. Then the world will know that you sent me and have loved them, even as you have loved me. (vs. 23)*

We witness that the shape of things has changed. The circles are no longer overlapping but instead are concentric.

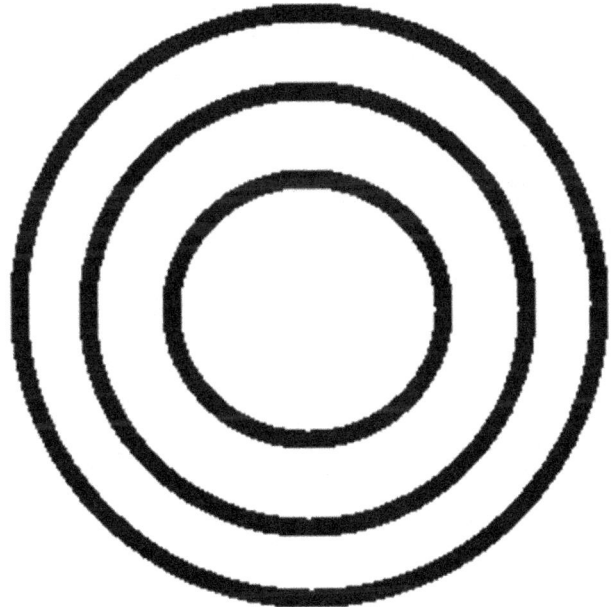

God is the circle within Jesus and Jesus is the circle within us (*I in them and you in me*)...full unity...each containing all of the other...there is no point of intersection but rather wholeness...a deep and abiding wholeness where one circle lives in relation to the other...Can you now see it? That one tear of compassion (the Spirit), falling from the face of Jesus as he sat in complete and utter anguish praying for us. Perhaps sensing how difficult it was going to be for us, how much of a challenge throwing off or turning away from patterns of this world would be, how the struggle and tension would linger on… all the while knowing what would soon be happening to himself. As I see it, the tear lands in the center of the circle (that is us) and if that center is some sort of barren desert then we will witness an explosion (revolution of self) that puts all the rest of our modern technological explosions to shame. This tear continues to be shed for anyone who is open to its reception. Explosions are the key! We are obsessed with them… violence, flames, the bigger the better. We all have deserts, they stretch for miles…

Quickly now, buckle yourself into the machine…we are catapulted into the sky…into space… and somehow float next to a descending tear, shrinking ourselves to size as we marvel at the undulating fluid mass as it reacts to the pressure of the air upon it… it has its struggles…its has its risks…but it finds its way.

So I ask you…Can you see it?

You know, that one tear…falling, landing, colliding, crashing onto the parched ground of a heart which is barely beating. Whether it lands on a stagnant pond or a dry desert, the results are the same…concentric rings ripple through space and begin to form an upward moving mass.

But the reasonable objections always come…a voice cries out, "The tear that lands in the desert just goes, 'thud', no explosion, no concentric rings…nothing but a small waft of dust, a wisp-o-wil, which drifts away…"

I don't know about you but this is where I like to go microscopic, it is here where the action is, watching the particles give away parts of themselves and change into something new…the violence…the collision, the landing of the tear can seem to last forever in slow motion!

So I ask you, can you see it?

The slow but sure rising up of the sand…the forming of the backward moving waves at the base of impact, the slow and necessary closing in on itself…it settles into calm…I wish there were more explosions.

There is part of us that watches our reason struggle and sometimes has mercy upon it.

This part of us **is** the tear from heaven that fell long ago and is at rest within each and every one of us…waiting to be noticed… waiting to help us experience the fullness of life…every time we turn our attention to it.

So often I want more…more than just some sort of lapse into silence…I want to not just reach out my open hands but rather to use my hands to hold some sort of hammer high all the while anticipating the way I will bring it crashing down upon something… anything…where I can see the sparks fly, and be amazed at my strength and control.

Quiet, silence, prayer, meditation…it is a different kind of upheaval…it denies our desire for sensory overload and challenges us to seek something far more lasting. God is always close to us, He is our divine center, it is right and good to believe in a transcendent God but it is also right to believe in a immanent God…as the ripples move outward so too may they move inward towards the center, our relation to God is the constant movement of love… if we allow ourselves to be porous to the Spirit.

Please be aware that I am not here trying to suggest the existence of or argue for the kind of unity that reason seems to sometimes either beg for or to dismiss as impossible but rather the unity that I see being expressed by the above verses is the kind that can never be known, captured or expressed by reason, it is a matter of deep and abiding love (faith)hidden in a cloud of unknowing...and yet very, very real.

We are not our Own

"What is it that Jesus the savior is doing? As we take in that question every day, our souls are nourished – even if we don't have the faintest clue about the answer because what we long for is not clarity but the God to whom we belong"[iii]

Our discussions about realizing our "closeness" to God and the fact that we need to learn to look within just as much as we look without do not come without presenting risks. As we become aware of the presence of God within and embrace the process of transformation we can, at times, become frustrated. Our value and dignity seem vouchsafed (no matter what we do) and our reliance on God to run the show can appear to leave us with not a whole lot to do… where is our involvement? Where is our action? What happens to us? How do we feel empowered? How can it be good for one to give up control? Is it right for me to get or take credit for my accomplishments and if not why does it seem to change my motivation so? These are the types of questions that can wage war with or derail our best intentions and it is right to want to search

---

iii M. Craig Barnes, Reclaiming the Heidelberg Catechism, Faith Alive Christian Resources, 2012 p156

out the kinds of conversations that can provide an adequate space for us to explore the comfort that quality answers can bring.

Several years ago I was introduced to the Heidelberg Catechism. It was written in 1563 at the direction of Fredrick III who ruled the province of the Palatinate which was located in the southern part of Germany. The palatinate referred to a section of territory that constituted an electorate for the Holy Roman Empire.

> *"At this time the palatinate, which encompassed Heidelberg, was divided between strict Lutherans sympathetic to Martin Luther and those Lutherans who preferred the changes Phillip Melanchthon had introduced to the churches. Still others were devoted to the Reformed teachings of John Calvin."*[5]

One of the main goals of the catechism was to bring these separate theological camps together by expressing that all of them held important beliefs in common.

> *"From the beginning it was clear that the Heidelberg Catechism was developed as a consensus document intended to relieve the anxiety of the people of the Palatinate. Not only were they anxious about their religious divisions, but beneath those pressing concerns lay the more profound anxieties of all humans: What holds life together? How do we know God? What is expected of a life well lived? And what will relieve us from our anxieties?"*[6]

These are obviously questions that can and are being asked in modern society as well. Although the authorship of the catechism is anonymous it is generally attributed to Zacharias Ursinus (a 28 year old theology professor) and Casper Olevianus (a 26year old pastor who had previously been a professor). Both of these men worked together with a team of other pastors and scholars to write a catechism for the people (average men and women) of the Palatinate. The construction of the catechism consists of 129 questions and answers. This question and answer format has always impressed me because it is as if the authors are saying that most people who are entering a church or trying to understand what it means to live a faithful life have questions and perhaps even some doubt and sometimes what they need most of all is the freedom to enter a conversation (a space) where questions are allowed, answers are suggested and guidance given. My purpose in introducing this catechism is not to do some sort of exhaustive analysis question by question but rather to bring to the forefront of our mind the importance of entering a conversation not just with our self but also with at least one other person (preferably a pastor or spiritual counselor) so we can learn the value of not only experiencing the honest struggle for truth that all of us on some level (unconscious/conscious) yearn for and deeply know but also how this struggle is reflected in another person's life as well. Yes, we are unique individuals trying to find our way but we also share this experience with others. It is when we acknowledge the presence of this shared struggle that we can see the true value of not just learning but also teaching (that we all have something valuable to share). "The point is not simply to recite the right answer, but to enter a holy conversation"[7] Question one of the catechism[iv] is the most famous and is often looked upon as a summary for the rest of the catechism and therefore it is this question (and answer) to which I would now like to direct our attention. Hopefully the results of our conversation here will easily be seen as readily applicable to our

---

[iv] Excerpts from catechism were taken from, Our Faith, Ecumenical Creeds, Reformed Confessions and other Resources, Faith Alive, Grand Rapids Michigan 2013.

continued examination of the closeness, process and simplicity of our relation to God.

Question - What is your only comfort in Life and in Death?
This question should draw the attention of us all!

*Answer – **That I am not my own**, but belong body and soul in life and in death to my faithful savior Jesus Christ. He has fully paid for all my sins with his precious blood, and has set me free from the tyranny of the devil. He also watches over me in such a way that not a hair can fall from my head without the will of my father in heaven: in fact, all things must work together for my salvation. Because I belong to him, Christ, by his Holy Spirit, assures me of eternal life and makes me wholeheartedly willing and ready from now on to live for him.*

On some level I immediately sense that I am on delicate ground here with many readers because of the highly formal or theological nature of the catechism. It is as if I have been walking along a path in the woods, looking for that elusive clearing (you know that place where everything comes together) but I have unexpectedly found myself sliding forward onto an ice covered pond…I can hear the alarming sound of cracking ice, tiny fissures forming in my only supporting surface. But I choose to press on…because I know not so much that Christ will carry me to the other side but rather that I am being invited not just to have a respectful conversation but to enter into a space, body and soul, where I can feel and be connected to the source of my being through the power of the Holy spirit. If I am going to find meaning anywhere it is in this space where I will find it.

The context of this first question needs to be noted because a person's reaction to it will vary greatly depending on the makeup of one's daily life. The person who is suffering in any way will react to it totally different than one who is not. My conclusion is that this catechism is not designed for those who see nothing wrong with life but rather for those that sense a certain kind of misery or tension…

the acknowledgment that something is missing, something has gone wrong. So I ask you,...What is your only comfort in Life and in Death?

That I am not my own

The words, "*that I am not my own*" strike a kind of deep and special chord which echoes within and demands my notice. What does it mean that I am not my own? How do I accept this notion and all the radical notions that follow from the above answer? I believe that part of the solution lies in the acknowledgment that in as much as there has been a great deal of change over the course of history concerning the mechanics of how we go about living our daily lives there has been little or no change in how we go about finding deep and lasting meaning or fulfillment. The letting go of ownership of our self is always a slow process full of fits and starts and retracing of steps but ultimately it is a struggle which is passed on from generation to generation. This process is discussed in the ancient wisdom of the mystics (St John of the Cross) as the overcoming of the false self (ego) and the discovery of our true self in God. It is also discussed by Paul in Ephesians 4:22, "*You were taught with regard to your former way of life, to put off your old self, which is being corrupted by its deceitful desires, to be made new in the attitude of your minds; and to put on the new self, created to be like God in true righteousness and holiness.*" The catechism its self also directly addresses this issue in question and answer 43. In response to the question, "What further advantage do we receive from Christ's sacrifice and death on the cross? The answer given is, "*Through Christ's death our old selves are crucified, put to death, and buried with him.*" We see that the old self or the conscious way that a person conceived of and related to the world dies. This death would necessarily consist in the transformation or renewing of a person's mind. But what does this really mean for us? This transformation comes with a deep awareness not just that "Christ paid for our sins" but that we have been rescued from our own self centered existence and one of the results is that there is now no need for us to feel as if we must earn our salvation. It is not earned but received in the absence of a personal sense of achievement. If we give up ownership of our self it means we belong to God, it means we are a child of God, it means that we open ourselves to feeling not just the presence of love in our life but the presence of a healthy parenting relationship which involves both love and guidance.

Therefore; the answer can no longer be for one to directly instruct another to "accept Jesus Christ as your Lord and Savior!" without being accompanied by a sense of invitation which holds up and celebrates not just the mystery and miracle of our relation to God but also the caring nature of this relation. This is the challenge...to express how this caring works itself out (or finds its way) in daily life. The presence of evil in this world is a significant obstacle to this challenge especially when it is being disseminated by a 24/7 media that seems hopelessly addicted to drama. It can inspire us all to question...why? But one of the things that it does not do is inspire people to take a step back and think about the larger arc of history. At the time this catechism was written the overall religious (and political...because religion and politics were combined) atmosphere was dominated by fear. This fear was in relation to judgment and the tyranny of a demonic world ruled by the devil and the hopelessness that a person would feel when they were told that they needed to somehow earn or pay (purchase indulgences) their way to heaven. One of the main motivations behind the Reform movement was the need to escape this hopeless situation. This escape began with the realization that if our old selves can be transformed or overcome then our lives no longer revolve around our self alone...

But belong body and soul in life and in death to my faithful savior Jesus Christ

Well, I have been out on the ice for a while now... the openness exposes me to the direct force of the wind. I have lost the ability to hide. In a way it can be comforting to know the truth but it also can be quite disconcerting because it involves something that seems foreign, something that I cannot quite grasp and hold in my hand so that I can feel and marvel at its beauty.

When I think about belonging to Christ "Body and soul in life and in death", I find that my thoughts usually go the incarnation of Christ. In dynamic one we talked about the mistaken tendency of some people to believe that they must transcend the world if they are to lead transformed or spiritual lives. If I belong to Christ, "body and soul" it means that Christ cares just as much about my daily life as he does about my afterlife in eternity. This is expressed by the fact that he chose to become human...and encourages us to follow his example and become fully human. One may want to question why there is such an emphasis put on daily life when we have already been encouraged to give up ownership of our self. It is here where I like to concentrate on the process of transformation. One way to see this process unfold is to take a look at things through the lens of "perspective". In dynamic one we talked about seeing things from the perspective which sees the incarnation of Christ as a way for us to see how to become fully human. When we discover that we are a child of God it is like we are standing out in the open, we know the truth and we now have a sense of freedom to look out at the world from all sorts of different perspectives and yet marvel at them all because they are unified by the truth of how we are a child existing in God's kingdom, body and soul, in this life and the next. We can see the expression of God...the face of God...in it all. On the other hand, if we are suffering from an addiction or in some way in need of recovery we often are seeing life from only one frozen perspective where we are the one with the problem, the whirlwind centers around us and somehow we will determine the only solution. There is no sense of freedom because we lack the following truth…

> *He has fully paid for our sins and set us free from the tyranny of the devil, and watches over us in such a way that not a hair can fall from our head without the will of our father in heaven.*

My intellectual side often wants to start out with a very basic question, "Why would Christ want to pay for my sins?" I don't get it. Even as a person in recovery I don't see myself as ever wanting to pay for another person's sins. But then I take a moment and think about my children and without question my outlook changes as I consider different circumstances in which I would perhaps find myself being willing to pay for their sins. When we think about the parenting relationship things change in terms of the willingness to make sacrifice. We need to incorporate this kind of parental willingness with the admission that of ourselves, as solitary points somehow floating in space and unconnected to anything greater than ourselves we are lacking an essential ingredient. Martin Luther who influenced the writing of the catechism through several visits to the Palatinate several years before the catechism was published, was frustrated by a religious and political atmosphere that was being run by fear instead of love and he also felt that he was somehow lacking that essential ingredient and without this ingredient it seemed impossible to him that he could ever succeed in a life of faith. Martin Luther found his answer in the book of Romans and with the apostle Paul he also began to champion the idea that the necessary missing ingredient is grace that comes through the Holy Spirit and brings to life the true caring nature of

God. It often remains difficult to see the Spirit at work in a world where evil is all too prevalent but yet the catechism insist

> *that not a hair can fall from our head without the will*
> *of our father in heaven.*

What does this mean in our modern world? That he allows us to be hurt? That he allows others to suffer? That he allows the agony of our and even his children? Once again we find our self out on the ice, perhaps hearing another crack or two, perhaps even falling to our hands and knees and peering intently into the ice looking for the depth that we need to support our weight. "Oh God, help me... help me not fall through!". We again stand and look for clues. If we have an open mind (heart) the arc of history can lead us in to an amazing answer. Evil has always been present in the world and in some ways was even more substantial, upfront and in your face with reference to the way people (at the time the catechism was written) were punished, tortured or executed in public squares etc... So often I think it is our language and reason that traps us in logical conundrums. If everything is God's will and evil is a part of everything than evil is God's will! We could begin a long parsing of words and logical analysis but I see this type of activity (however tempting it is) as a fool's errand. The problem of evil has always existed, there is nothing new about it whatsoever but there is also nothing new concerning how a person can find meaning and fulfillment even in our modern times. The answer that comes from history (and the catechism) concerning evil is precisely this,

> *that all things work together for our salvation.*

In truth, there is a part of me that responds by saying, "really... is the really the case?"...but then I am able to notice a kind of rising wave (an upward moving mass) which allows me to see things from the different perspective or vantage point of faith and it is faith that allows me to see the wonderful puzzle of light which makes up this world and make the necessary conclusion that the world is somehow incomplete without each and every one of us in it as we all somehow perform a necessary function. As we begin to feel the presence of God, the caring presence of God, our focus can be lifted from heartache, pain and grief and transformed into joy. Why? Because we have found the missing ingredient of grace. It is grace which allows us not to dismiss the presence of evil but to bare its weight as something which is always outmatched by something greater. In the final analysis I think we need to say that God does indeed allow bad things to happen but that the initiation of these events is indeterminate and almost certainly initiated at times by the human will alone. We all know that great goodness can come from great suffering but if we can begin to see the nurturing and caring presence of the hand of God in all that we do we can also see that this presence always promotes love at the expense of evil and we can say together...

> *Because I belong to him, Christ, by his holy spirit assures me of eternal life and makes me wholeheartedly willing and ready from now on to live for Him.*

We have been talking about coming to terms with the issue of evil and getting to know the nurturing, caring presence of God (the Holy Spirit) and for me all of this is overshadowed by the repeating notion or echo *"that we are not our own".* We are reminded that this answer is in response to the question, *"What is your only comfort in life and in death?"*

I think many people balk at the notion of eternal life and even more balk (or at least fear or feel anxious about) at the notion of eternal judgment. It is a difficult subject because we obviously know nothing about it. So then how does the Holy Spirit assure us of eternal life and how does this affect the whole notion of judgment?

The way that I like to address this question is to focus on the way in which our salvation has undoubtedly already begun in the now. The way we can begin to feel the comfort and assurance that the Holy Spirit can give as it manifests itself in the gift of faith. It is this undeserved gift of faith through sheer grace that allows us to feel the presence of the Holy Spirit in our life and the actions that it inspires within. It is the blessing or condition of faith lived out through gratitude in action which cannot help but nurture a sense of hope for what awaits us in eternity.

So now, by the grace of God, I have shuffled half way across the frozen pond and made my way onto the solid ground of a small island. Here I learn to rest upon the solid ground of faith; this becomes my rock and my refuge.

The idea of a judging God has turned many people away from faith and in my experience this is usually connected to a deep seated resentment because of a strict church upbringing which seemed to them (sometimes rightly) to focus exclusively on the judgment of God at the expense of his love. In their eyes they were never introduced to a loving and caring God. The Heidelberg Catechism seems to go out of its way to impress upon the reader how Christ has paid the price for our sin and how this act in itself should release us from our concern for judgment. I genuinely believe that throughout the question and answer process we can become aware of a space into which we are being invited to enter and it is here in this space that we can take the forgiveness of our sins into our heart and in a sense be reborn as one who is grafted into Christ. This grafting into Christ changes who we are and allows us to live a life that is absent of the fear of judgment but yet a life that still knows the struggle against sin. We are always in the human condition but yet this same human condition allows for our steady progression into a life of faith. If there is a God what would it be like to not be near him? Do we perhaps know something of this feeling already? It seems that although God is a loving God, if we choose to grow distant, if we choose to turn or move away from him he does not stop us. I sometimes wonder what it would be like if after living a life here on earth we were introduced to a loving God whom we had never come to know but yet all of the sudden did…there is something in this thought of confrontation which carries great weight… perhaps it is about a sense of fear but I think more rightly it is about sensing the truth about the space into we are being invited to enter.

But by no means, do I no longer have questions, the conversation always continues on…

What do you believe concerning the Holy Spirit?[v]

> *First, he as well as the Father and the Son is eternal God. Second he has been given to me personally, so that by true faith, he makes me share in Christ and all his blessings, comforts me, and remains with me forever.*

This is a personal God, working through his son who in turn is working through the Holy Spirit; this is a father (or parent) who has been given (gifted) to us. However much we may feel we are undeserving, however much we may feel that we cannot surrender our center to anyone except our self, God's hand will always remain open and outstretched. He stands on the shore (the edge of the pond) and says, "Come follow me and I will make you fishers of men." Matt 4:19. We can experience this gift (this embrace of the father) as faith and in so doing we can share in the blessings of

---

[v] I am using Q&A 53 from the catechism to emphasize not just the personal nature of our relation to God but the key role of the Spirit who remains with us forever.

Christ. These blessings are the comfort and assurance that can come from the acknowledgment that each one of us can indeed have a personal and heartfelt relationship with God.

I sense and Hope that we all have made it to the other side of the pond and if indeed we have we will often be surprised by what we see. We are no longer in "Kansas" anymore... we are no longer taking a stroll through the woods. The task or challenge has now become to take this notion of a spirit driven faith and apply it to our daily life which can at times be overwhelmed by what seems like an ever changing complex world which doesn't seem to foster becoming connected to a power greater than ourselves. Our focus is often drawn to more worldly things and in our haste to acquire these things, including what we see as forms of success both in and outside of recovery, we sometimes find our self frustrated because of a perceived lack of progress and thus we find ourselves in need of a different perspective.

Dynamic Two – Stagnation vs Process

This dynamic reflects what I see when a person's recovery slows to a crawl and it lacks a sense of vitality for those who, in essence, no longer feel as if they are growing. Yes they still want to go to meetings, yes they recognize the necessity of talking with and helping others (and sometimes this even makes them feel better) but in general there is a malaise or sense of boredom that forms a certain kind of backdrop to their life in recovery. Boredom has always carried a certain sense of importance to me because I realized that it was one of the major reasons I drank…this felt sense of boredom or emptiness. In a book called, "How not to be Secular", James K. A. Smith indicates that what most threatens a modern person's sense of self-sufficiency is boredom or the fear of boredom. Having nothing to do introduces us to the spectre of meaninglessness. *"And it is precisely our unhappiness, our restlessness in these conditions that give us a desire to gather together the scattered moments of meaning into some kind of whole".* So in other words if we face our boredom in a healthy manner we can realize how it is calling us to a deeper understanding of our self as a human being. We also can take notice of the way society defines success through wealth, productivity and efficiency as opposed to wholeness or fullness. With these observations in hand we can begin to make an initial investigation into what it is that truly governs our choices.

> *"To say the least, the balance between habit and freedom is delicate. We must bear full responsibility for choosing among our loves thousands of times each day, but our options are limited and often out of our control. If this were all there were to life, it would be impossible and hardly worth it. But there is more to life than choosing among loves. There is a single larger choice that can breathe freedom and spontaneity into every decision, every moment."*[8]

As our lives play out we are determined by what we choose to love but the key factor is when we realize that our choices of love are but a corrupted fraction of a much greater love of which we are constantly being invited to learn ever more.

In the book, The Awakened Heart, Gerald May continues on to share the experience of Dag Hammarskjold (former United Nations Secretary and Nobel Peace laureate)

> *"I don't know Who or What put the question. I don't know when it was put. I don't even remember answering. But at some moment I did answer Yes to Someone or Something and from that hour I was certain that existence is meaningful and that, therefore my life, in self surrender had a goal."*[9]

Mr. Hammarskjold was sharing his experience of surrendering to the power of love but more importantly he was expressing how surrendering to the larger invitation of love is very different as compared to the way we often choose among our loves in order to get through our days. Love in this lower sense is the emotion we invest in the material things of this world.

"Life goes on, struggles continue and the Yes is continually re-invited. Saying, Yes to love does not make our problems go away, it can however give us a vision for what our problems are for and why our struggles have value beyond efficiency."[10]

As we reflect on this higher and lower form of love it can bring a sense of reality to the acknowledgment that we do indeed exhibit a kind of struggle which doubts the choices we sometimes make but presses on, coldly believing we are doing what needs to be done.

For in my inner being I delight in God's law but I see another law at work within me waging war against the law of my mind and making me a prisoner of the law of sin that is at work within me. Rom 7:22-23

Upon first reading the above verse one may be struck by the darkness or negativity with which Paul is speaking but in my mind the real message behind these words is not how one needs to feel how they have been defeated by their brokenness but rather in realizing the importance of turning one's attention to the parts of our self that are in tension. If anything is going to change, this awareness of tension is the first thing that needs to happen. We recognize that something is wrong. Early on in my recovery it was not just about recognizing that I was selfish and self centered but it was also about recognizing a deep seated anger that I had toward not only the world but also toward God who I felt had more or less abandoned myself and the world to our own devices. It took a good long while to recognize this as representative of a certain kind of tension between living a life directed solely on self will and living a life guided by the will of God.

I have often thought that repeated abuse of alcohol and drugs carries with it at least an unconscious admission that something has gone terribly wrong... that the horizon (*you know when we look off into the distance and wonder about things*) of life and the way in which ultimate meaning is to be connected with one's life have somehow shifted or at least have become very confusing or vague. Finding meaning by executing daily life better than anyone else has long since ceased to be an option and fitting into a religious frame of reference is an option that comes with many choices... and in this simple fact alone sits all the anxiety one needs to wildly grow frustration.

In addition, I believe that many people who are early on in their recovery (*and beyond*) share a common trait and that is that they take them self very seriously (*this is another way of saying we are perfectionist*). Failure destroyed us as we repeatedly went through times when we just couldn't succeed under our own will power and as result we felt hopeless. Because of our repeated failure in controlling our life, we became stuck in some sort of cycle which brought with it stagnation and the endless cycle of attachment and addiction. Everything was spinning out of control and as much as we wanted to reach out and somehow grab hold of everything that was spinning around us (*the whirlwind, tempest, storm*) we simply could not.

Once we begin to live from a divine center (*that was introduced in dynamic one*), things change and one of the primary things that changes is an individual's sense of self worth or value. If a person's value comes from God than it is not something that disappears when one experiences failure but rather it becomes the constant that allows one to press on through failure, knowing all the while that their core sense of value remains unchallenged. Daily life now becomes a place where God belongs and where his presence is felt. We respond by realizing that life is a process, a process of learning how to identify and address the tension of the Christian life and I think that this is precisely what recovery is. Yes we have been set free from the power of sin but we are not sinless. When I think about the law of sin I think about a continuum which stretches across the many deserts of our minds *(yes, I know that chemicals crossing synapses produce thought or vice versa…but when I am in reflection I don't see chemicals, I see an endless kind of space which puts any kind of man made video to shame, mystery and miracle always comes to mind)* where the sometimes complicated decisions of our daily lives play out…just because I stopped drinking doesn't mean that I stopped sinning. We are always being challenged to allow ourselves to be led by the Spirit *(our divine center)* but we often fail in this regard and find ourselves succumbing to the temptations of our inner deserts. So often this struggle with sin does not express itself in some sort of great conflict with each decision a person makes but rather with a much more basic turning away from God. We either choose to simply not look at the rays of light (grace) coming through the window *(our heart?)* or we take the light for granted…it hardly demands our notice. This is the kind of tension that Paul noticed within himself, "waging war against the law of his mind." It is Paul's deep recognition of this tension that allows him to provide the answer, "the law of the Spirit who gives life has set you free from the law of sin and death." (Rom 8: 2)

Hope is born in the acknowledgment of the presence of the Spirit. With grace (from and through the Spirit) we can gradually begin to see that life is not just about what I can do under my own will power but rather about nurturing a relationship with something except myself. For anyone who is trying to lead a Christian life and who is familiar with bible history, they know the history of Adam and they know the history of Christ and that something incredible has happened, there has been this great shift between the old and the new aeon and that Christ has delivered us from the power of sin. There is a great theological theme that underlies this awareness and that is that the kingdom of God has indeed come but it is also not yet fulfilled. In the mean time we are left in our human condition (where tension remains) but we have not been left without hope as the Spirit of Christ that is within us enables us to overcome and persevere in the Christian life. In chapter 3 of Ephesians Paul writes, "*I pray that out of his glorious riches he may strengthen you with power through his Spirit in your inner being, so that Christ may dwell in your hearts through faith.*" We cannot conjure up or create faith but when we reflect on and begin to live as one who stops resisting the influence of our divine center we "begin to see" how the intimate awareness of the Spirit who resides within nurtures and sustains the gift of faith. I guess if God wanted, this could happen in a flash, in a grace filled moment of time and as a matter of fact I think that this does happen in moments but unfortunately the moments are just that, moments…and they pass…these moments are real and powerful and can bring about healing (*the increasing of love*) but the experience of my life has also told me that we are "in process"… that we are in the process, "of becoming" a child of God. The entire world in which we live seems to be built on efficiency (*in many forms*) and this outlook militates against the slow and sometimes awkward process of becoming a child of God but it is this process that will give us the answers we truly desire especially in relation to why we exist and how we should use our lives.

As I recall the person that I was when I first entered recovery I would have found it very difficult to tolerate an abundance of scripture based spiritual advice and the reason for this was my ironic belief in my own ability to come to a reasonable realistic understanding of things (even though my life experience did not back up or confirm this ability). There is no doubt that I missed God, there is no doubt that I experienced a sense of grieving for the world and myself but I was also governed by a certain belief that said that the real cause of my healing would come from understanding what had gone wrong and making corrections through my own effort alone. Every time I have felt my life slowing down to a crawl (and thereby stagnating) this notion is somehow involved. If we truly want to experience freedom we need to wrestle most of all with our need to run the show. This does not mean that we do not put effort into guiding our lives in a certain direction but rather that we incorporate the possibility of failure as something that is part of a process in learning how to develop a healthy and personal relationship with God.

The Pond

The idea of finding a way to describe the inner workings of the mind in a down to earth way has always intrigued me. When I stand back and reflect on this process I cannot help but be amazed that the organ inside our skull, in seemingly perfect coordination with our bodies, is capable of not only managing the day to day, moment to moment, operation of our physical body but also can imagine some of the most wondrous scenes and somehow "see" them within our own mind. To me this is one of the outstanding miracles of life which we all too often seem to take for granted.

Now I firmly realize that a discussion of the operation of the human mind is beyond the scope of a book about how to facilitate the process of recovery but I do think that looking at or considering the operation of the mind from a metaphorical perspective can help each one of us have a better appreciation of what it is that we indeed call Life and this appreciation can in turn help us to address periods of stagnation as we remember that we are part of the unfolding process of transformation.

The metaphor that I would like to consider is that of a pond. I prefer using the idea of a pond as opposed to a lake or ocean because a pond seems more personal or individual. It is an undeniable fact that our minds are individual circles unto themselves, we do not have the ability to enter or truly know the inner workings of another person's mind. A pond is a small body of water that has been gathered unto its self and we normally can see only the surface even though there is without a doubt much going on in the depths. A great deal of what goes on in the depths of our mind is attributed to the automatic or unconscious regulation of biological demands. There is although a large amount of inherited material passed on from a long line of relations. So too, ponds are often fed by a number of different streams. Their small size seems to limit their capacity but even a small pool of water can have an amazing affect on the life around it. Our minds may be circles unto themselves but it is our relationships with others that allow us to have an effect on the inner workings of another's mind.

About a year and half ago I was visiting my son and his wife as they had recently experienced the birth of their son. As I was holding my grandson and looking into his content and happy eyes I was truly amazed. I was holding him up and in front of me, one hand under each shoulder and as I lowered him down upon my lap his legs would react and push upward as his body was naturally responding to the outside world. During this same time period I was in the process of completing some seminary classes which had reinforced in me an already keen interest in the "soul". I can remember briefly explaining this interest to my son and giving particular attention to how I was fascinated by the inter connection of the heart, mind, body and soul. It had occurred to me as I was holding my grandson that the real person I should be having this conversation with was in fact the baby himself because he of course, at this time, (especially when seen through the lens of a grandfather's eyes) was "all soul". It is amazing to look at happy content infants blissfully unaware of themselves, living completely for the moment that is before them...but yet they do not lack depth...there is an immensity of depth and they float in it freely for they have not yet become fixated on creating their surface dwelling or the frame or structure through which they will view and interact with the world and individuals in it.

This observation hints at the idea that our soul is much more than just our sense of awareness and that if we are going to try and equate the soul with consciousness or mind, as is often done through a study of scripture[vi], than we must make sure that we define consciousness as something that is much more than just our sense of self awareness but rather as some kind of indescribable diamond or stone that has an infinite number of facets which are being continually revealed and perhaps even remade and created anew as we experience life. So when we think or reflect on the presence of soul it does seem appropriate that we indeed see it as the breath of God which is not some kind of thing or piece of matter that can be analyzed to the nth degree.

> *"The Lord God formed a man from the dust of the ground and breathed into his nostrils the breath of life, and the man became a living being."* Gen 2:7

In the book, "The Human Phenomenon" by Teilhard de Chardin, the author asks a simple question, "Why is it that we are not more sensitive to the presence of something on the move at the heart of us that is greater than ourselves?...a reality that seeks itself among a world of groping forms."[11] Teilhard de Chardin was a Jesuit priest who was also a paleontologist and he dedicated a large portion of his life to studying the evolution of man. Now it is clear that the topic of evolution can still be controversial for some but I also feel that Tielhard de Chardin is able to hold evolution up to the light in such a way that the breath of God is never questioned but rather the key to understanding its overarching purpose. As an example he stresses that, "The human came into the world

---

[vi] Please see https://www.gci.org/spiritual/soulspirit

silently."[12] Tielhard spent years studying skeletons of primitive man but yet he also knew that skeletons in themselves would never tell him about the advent of consciousness. Whether or not one believes in evolution or in the garden of Adam and Eve the miracle for humanity is the same…it is the moment that God breathes life into us in a way which allows us to reflect upon ourselves. The main thing that separates humans from animals in terms of the operation of their mind is that the human mind seems to have an inner dimension where the birth of self awareness takes place and is signified by the ability to "see" not only in a physical way but also in a mental and perhaps even spiritual way. As humans we can see and peer into the depths of ourselves in a way which animals cannot.

So I hope that we all can at least imagine ourselves standing next to a pond, perhaps on a hill under the shade of a tree…we see the perfectly still crystal clear surface and we marvel at the accuracy of reflections, the upside down trees on the surface almost appear to be the very roots of the trees themselves which have been laid bare for all to see. The wind blows and they are taken away but their presence always comes back when calm returns. Everything seems to happen on the surface but yet we know there is activity below, some of these depths have never been seen. We begin to concentrate on these areas, we realize the pond after all is part of who we are and as we peer into the depths we witness the rising up of some sort of solid ground…a sort of island where thoughts and ideas come to the light of day. We are of course present with these thoughts… some of them are strangers but yet also somehow closer to us than anything else could be. Spending time on this island or place of reflection can be challenging, we can make it vanish in an instant, this of course is part of the powers of our mind but we also have the opportunity to learn as we watch our self struggle, you know from the safety of the shade from the tree on the hill. There are different ways to live, we can simply watch and marvel at the surface of things, we can create islands of thought which we make appear and vanish at will or we can begin to realize how the depths of our life always rise up one way or another. Even if we remain steadfast in dedicating our lives to the surface of things the depths will rise up and cast something upon the unsuspecting shore. Usually it will involve some type of suffering which will often take us on a slow and painstaking journey of hopefully learning some kind of acceptance and perhaps being reminded of the importance of connecting our self to that which is on the move at the heart of us. But if we try and cultivate an appreciation for supporting and watching ourselves struggle we can keep an island or at least a relevant sense of awareness that our lives "are not our own" but are gifted to us and that somehow when we begin the journey, when we dive deep into the discovery of who we are we find God. And it is this "finding" which connects us to a power that can walk with us through everything.

> "From our flaws flows the need for help. Spirituality suggests that the first prayer is a scream, a cry for help. O God come to my assistance, O Lord make haste to help me (Psalm 70), sung for over a millennium and a half at the beginning of each monastic hour. The insight is constant: Our darkness is a thirst for God, the Spiritual for whatever might alleviate this painful side of the human condition, We seek help for what we cannot face or accomplish alone; in seeking help we accept and admit our own powerlessness. And that acceptance and admission, in the acknowledgment that we are not in control, spirituality is born."[13]

So what I am hopefully doing in suggesting that the cultivation of an island of reflection is beneficial in the process of recovery and by extension also the business of being a human being, is to try and encourage a new perspective from which to see God as the center from and around which our consciousness revolves. The pond of our mind is more than just a surface which is at the mercy of the elements waiting for a wind which comes from a place which we know not whence. Our consciousness holds something to be discovered and what this something is can sometimes be glimpsed by holding a happy and content infant who is blissfully living in the moment.

"Truly I tell you, unless you become like a child you will never enter the kingdom of heaven." (Matt 18:3).

Yet, there is a part of us that objects, which cries out, "but an infant does not think… an infant does not reflect…an infant is not yet self aware…but we are!…there has got to be something good about becoming self aware right? Yes, there is something good about being self aware and all the good advancements of technology which are rooted in our ability to reflect upon ourselves testify to this but the main point of emphasis here is that our self awareness does not stand alone but rather is only part of a consciousness which also involves a mind, heart and body and our task is to strive to bring these different aspects of our consciousness into balance. As we come to know ourselves more completely we will at times wrestle with frustration as the way forward is not always clear.

> "*The core paradox that underlies Spirituality is the haunting sense of incompleteness, of being somehow unfinished, that comes from the reality of living on this earth as part and yet also not part of it. For to be human is to be incomplete, yet yearn for completion; it is to be uncertain, yet long for certainty; to be imperfect, yet long for perfection; to be broken, yet crave wholeness. All the cravings remain necessarily unsatisfied, for perfection, completion, certainty and*

wholeness are impossible precisely because we are imperfectly human. This is the essential paradox of human life: We are always and inevitably incomplete, on the way, slipping and sliding making mistakes. But the ancient voices insist that this is not failure: it is rather the necessary reflection of the paradox that we are. Paradox is the way it was meant to be."[14]

The answer is found in recognizing what is on the move at the heart of us.

The answer is in letting this engender and reinforce a growing faith that gives rise to a sense of joy that permeates our life.

It is most definitely a process.

The Gladiator Ring and the Gaming Sphere

"Almost none of us liked the self searching, the leveling of our pride, the confession of shortcoming which the process requires for its successful consummation." [vii]

Now that we have spent some time becoming familiar with the notion that we have an inner world that needs to be kept in balance I thought that it would be appropriate to make sure I was presenting a realistic picture of not only the difficult nature of the process into which we all have been invited but also how this process really is dominated by a part of ourselves that can sometimes hold another part of ourselves back.

There is clearly a part of us that questions things and I think we would be hard pressed to say that this part is mistaken in its operation. It would seem that many things that are set before us on a daily basis need to be questioned as to their value in terms of contributing to our lives in a healthy way. I would even go so far as to say that in today's modern world people not only yearn for meaning but we also yearn for a simpler time when we were not being presented with so many conflicting or alternative viewpoints.

[vii] Alcoholics Anonymous, *There is a Solution*, 3rd ed, AA World Services, 1976, p25

Psychology (as a Science) explains our conception of right and wrong as being related to or born from our physical experience of pain and pleasure. We gradually come to understand this experience as we use our reason to create a working knowledge of the difference between right and wrong. In a general way it seems that we are taught that our conscience (the abstract place where we decide what is right and wrong through some sort of debate) is subject to reason. And in this singular fact we are introduced to the main source for most of the intellectual conflict (related to morality and meaning) that a person can experience. It goes without saying that all people allow their reason or intellect to influence their decision making. I would be foolish to try and suggest that this should not be the case but I would like to put forward the notion that I would also be foolish to suggest that intellect and reason should be the only thing from which our guidance in decision making should come.

The discussion of the creation and operation of the conscience is a huge topic and attempting to confirm or deny one theory over another is not what I would see as being of benefit to our engagement of the dynamics of recovery but what can be of use to this engagement is developing an awareness of the relationship which exist between reason and the conscience. In order to do this we need a metaphor and I would like to begin by suggesting the use of "the gladiator ring".

Throughout my young adulthood and into midlife I would say that I often had a passional side that would seek excitement just as much as peace and contentment but I also had developed what I would call an allegiance to reason. Years later, after I had entered recovery, I began to reflect on this allegiance and I saw it as a kind of presence that I would call my "self" but yet it always seemed to be at odds with another part of my "self" or what I might call my emotional (gut level) side. More than anything else I began to realize that my intellectual side was completely dominating my emotional side and in addition I thought that this was necessary and good. As I became more aware of this imbalance I more or less started a mental war and my conscience became a place occupied by a great amount of debate. (*Concerning things like the existence of God, the true meaning of freedom, the nature of evil in the world, the role of the human will in accomplishing whatever we set our minds to etc...*)

The metaphor of the gladiator ring seems appropriate because it is a place where a distinct struggle can be seen (or imagined) between the true and false self with particular emphasis on philosophical argument (questions of meaning) within one's own mind. I saw the ring itself as my conscience, it was not some sort of fixed entity which was white and pure but it was a place that could become stained (with blood), it could become changed in negative ways. If I felt that it was being changed in a negative way it was because I was not working out the philosophical problems in the hopeful positive way that my heart was always guiding me towards and therefore it could be a place and cause of anxiety. I would always imagine two gladiators (symbolic of the opposite sides of an argument) entering the sand covered ring and fighting to the point of exhaustion and then for some reason "shaking hands" until they came back the following day to start the process again. In the background of this conception there were two assumptions. First, there was something noble about the process of coming to a draw and shaking hands only to continue the fight another day and second that the gladiator's were honorable and would only fight to the point of exhaustion and not death. I have since realized that the second option is dubious or naive therefore I had to realize the necessity of recasting this metaphor into what I like to call the "the gaming sphere". In essence, I realized that I had baked in the fact that there was no real cost (except for temporary anxiety until I found the next answer), there was no real risk of loss when doing thoughtful battle and that somehow this is the proper way to live a reasonable life of conscience. Neither metaphor is an adequate representation of what our conscience truly is and the way these metaphors reflect my experience is undoubtedly different than the readers but I believe that the gaming sphere (as a metaphor) can be more readily used to show how decisions of conscience and the process of leading a reflective life can be overwhelmed by our modern tendencies toward distraction and learned indifference because of what seems like a never ending complex parade of alternative viewpoints. What follows is my attempt to explain what this "gaming sphere" means for us today, especially with reference to our conception of our conscience, and I will suggest that the although the internet is undoubtedly a tool of progress it at least provides an atmosphere which not only reinforces the "gaming sphere" but also makes us vulnerable to manipulation (**especially in terms of politics**) as we search for frames through which to see and understand our world and especially our place in it. Finally I will relate this to the human condition with particular emphasis on what the Old Testament can bring to bear on this current predicament.

The gaming sphere essentially relates to my observation that modern people whether well educated or not can begin to realize that given the proper information almost any argument, especially in relation to philosophical ideas, can be pummeled into an infinite regression where a standoff between two opposing sides seems to be the inevitable conclusion. Reflection becomes a process that is not about getting to a definite answer but rather about getting to a position from which one can at least obtain the feeling of belonging to a group of like minded people. This being the case it can leave a person who attaches extreme importance to absolute certainty in a state of anxiety. This anxiety can be overcome by the courage of faith which sees doubt as an honest starting point or invitation to explore our relation to God (especially through scripture) but more often than not we have a different phenomenon taking place. The average man or woman does not seem to engage nor see the importance of engaging "life questions in relation to meaning" on a **conscious** level.

Now, we should note that a healthy normal average person is usually not walking around frustrated by philosophical conundrums (at least not consciously) nor sitting on the internet trying to find answers to these very same questions. The average person typically uses the internet as a surface level tool to make life easier or more efficient and this is not a bad thing. It is used for paying bills, shopping, news and entertainment and if perchance an individual wants to have a certain point of view confirmed or denied they can look for supporting evidence etc.... The gaming sphere for the average person comes into existence when he or she learns or becomes inwardly aware of the overwhelming ocean of information that the internet and world represents and how the they cannot ever come close to being able to process it all...**and that this is OK** and that it is something that they can just be acknowledged with a kind of **brushing glance** and then one moves on just as in the case with playing a game, the loss of certainty is not significant because it comes with no perceivable cost. The ocean of information creates a climate in which almost any point of view can be confirmed (on a surface level), sexual preference, political ideology, racism, etc... Within the gaming sphere we are allowed (options) to either make an admission of defeat (*I don't want to play*) followed by, "*Just leave me alone, I am choosing to exit the game*" or "*just tell me what I need to know and I will accept it without question*" or a willful use of the internet to confirm only what one wants to be told "*I will play, but only on my terms and I will stack the deck*".

The use of technology for fantasy application emphasizes the extent to which distraction from that which is overwhelming (the fear of boredom) in favor of having one's mind being intensely occupied has become highly valued. I find it tempting to say that this valuing of distraction is built upon a learned indifference to questions of meaning but I firmly believe that on some level we all care about meaning. The problem is how this concern with ultimate meaning has been demoted or has been somehow relegated to something which is at work within our unconscious alone where it can influence our susceptibility to addiction.

Because the internet has become a single "hub" or "router" to which the entire world directs its attention it necessarily places incredible power in the hands of a very few people especially when we compare the number of people who decide what information gets placed on home pages to the number of people who are accessing them etc…This in turn creates a situation in which people become vulnerable to manipulation. I guess a lot of people would say that this is very obvious and nothing new at all, that people have been manipulated by those in power throughout history and to this I would have to agree. What is new is the distance, the level of separation that is felt between one's country (world, universe) and the individual (the self) and this is being born out in the absolute frustration that the American public is demonstrating with reference to politics. The disconnect between politicians and the common man is monstrous. (Let's give them the benefit of the doubt here) This monstrosity is not because of the lack of concern for the common man by elected officials but rather because of the growing complexity of our changing world.

One way to look at it would be that there are two paces of change. The pace of change in politics is at a snail's pace while the pace of change in modernity is mind blowing. In many ways the politicians are just trying to hang on to their jobs but at the same time they are getting reams of information that the public is not and they must not only try to make good decisions but must also sort out whether or not they themselves are vulnerable to being manipulated (they too are being challenged to make real decisions of conscience). In dynamic one we talked about the intentional distant relationship that many people in recovery (and elsewhere) have with God. How does this distance relate to the distance that an individual can also feel towards one's country etc…? The answer is that the distance that a citizen feels from their country can at times intensify the need to "be their own center". It intensifies the need to defend the self, the independent ego that is in control and ever marching forward. At least until they get to the point of surrender. But if a person has already in a sense checked out of the pursuit of questions of meaning and no longer engages struggles of conscience on a conscious level and instead hangs out in the gaming sphere only when something goes wrong and stays only long enough to get a few tidbits of information in order to defend this or that position, how do they ever get to the point of surrender?

The best answer I have found comes from scripture and it drives home the point that there is a clear separation between the mind (reason), heart, and conscience. "*They show that the requirements of the law are written on their hearts, their consciences also bearing witness, and their thoughts sometimes accusing them and at other times defending them.*" Rom 2:15. Within this letter to the Romans Paul is here trying to communicate the necessary message that both Jews and Gentiles are sinners and in need of salvation. He is cautioning the Jews to not judge the Gentiles too harshly because they themselves are sinners and in some cases the Gentiles, who are without the written law, are doing a better job of obeying the law because it is written on their hearts. What this is showing us, in my opinion, is that in the final analysis, yes we do have and should use reason, yes we do have and should use our conscience but we also have something else and that is our heart and our heart contains not an avenue to pure reason but the advocate of the Spirit (*Gal 4:6, John 16:7,15*). This of course can get greatly confused by popular phrases like, "the heart wants what the heart wants" with reference to romance etc...but the key here is to realize the presence that we have within...that is not us... but something gifted to us and through prayer and study we can come to know it and depend on it as we develop a heartfelt relation to it. So often we can see the conscience as a place of reason and debate and not at all a place where the Spirit can have a say and when we subtract the Spirit we subtract too much. Our true conscience is not just a place where our reason is battling our emotion but rather a place where our mind and our conscience can be unified by what is in our heart.

By rectifying the two paces of change in "politics vs modernity" mentioned above we can begin to see it as an atmosphere in which the Spirit is indeed at work. We can clarify things by seeing this as a comparison between the speed of scientific change (modernity) and the speed of change (or the ingrained resistance to change, as we see in politics) within the individual. The first question would be are they truly different? We could also ask is the change real in so far as it represents actual change concerning fundamental behavior of human beings (are we improving morally)? The answer to both I believe is Yes...change is real and in some ways overall world morality is improving from a macroscopic perspective but we are still greatly flawed and the speed of scientific change is far greater than the change an individual encounters, in some cases individuals prefer the least amount of change possible.

This difference in preference for speed of change can be explained by using a concept which has been well tested by time, **the human condition**. Some would say that the human condition is about our fallen nature, brokenness, existential angst or an inability to satisfy our desire for unity or wholeness (with a power greater than ourselves, our absolute source of origin, the prime mover). When I imagine these topics being presented to a roomful of average men or women of a secular nature (*and who have become accustomed to spending time in the gaming sphere*) I see looks of bewilderment accompanied by comments like, "I'm not broken, I'm happy, what in the world is existential angst, just give me enough money to pay the bills and enough food on my family's table and I'm good." This brings to mind the realization that many people already exist in or have disengaged mental outlooks which say, "listen I don't need to understand anything more than what I already know, I have a philosophy of life, although I don't call it that, which allows me to be content with what I have, there is no call for me to enter into the fray of things (have struggles of conscience) I don't and cannot understand furthermore I don't have any need to get involved in any cause to help save the world because I am busy with what I already need to do to make ends meet and I am OK with that, Amen!" So what does this do for the topic of the human condition? Has it been shot into oblivion, all its particles slowly fading off into space? Does the human condition no longer exist? This requires a basic answer... the human condition does in fact exist and no it is not on some kind of continuum but it is in fact something that is experienced depending on the circumstances of one's life. Suffering accentuates the experience of the human condition.

Let's take the example of the Israelites. Wondering about in the desert being reminded of their God's existence by the periodic miracles which he would perform which allowed their survival (manna from heaven, water from rocks, flocks of birds (much needed meat) which dropped like rain) when things got rough and they were **suffering** but as things got better they would again doubt His existence despite these previous miracles and once again begin the worship of idols. Although the argument could easily be made that we have fallen back into the worship of idols in modernity, I am not trying to reinforce this view rather what I want to bring our attention to is the way that suffering wakes us up to the fact that healing is needed and that most of all healing is something that is done unto us and that it is not something that we can ever manufacture. Yes, we invent drugs, yes we administer vaccines, yes we want to take credit for the accomplishments of humanity but if we allow ourselves to look deeper still (deep calls to deep) we can see that we are only providing or improving the surface on which the miracle of healing takes place. The surgeon closes the wound but the process of healing is something all together different. This is the only way that the human condition can be addressed which underlines the absolute necessity of grace (the author of true healing). Although the human condition is generally associated with one's brokenness it would be an incomplete assessment if we did not also mention the positive side of the human condition which can be seen through the lens of unitive moments. At one time or another it would seem that all human beings exhibit a sense of awe relating to the beauty they find in a natural scene or a work of art. We sense the presence of peace in an infant's ability to truly live in the moment or a toddler's natural desire to show compassion and empathy. These feelings of awe and appreciation signal our ongoing ability to sense His presence regardless of our human condition. Despite all the change that has taken place since the time of the Israelites journey in the desert our relationship to God remains unchanged. It is right and proper to admit and perhaps even pray…

Father, God almighty
  All the change in the world is OK
  Be my constant,
  Be my rock,
  Be my refuge,
  Be the place of rest from which I can put it all in **perspective***.*
Amen.

It is important to note that even when the Israelites finally exited the desert into the land of Canaan and would experience the reigns of king David and king Solomon these times were not without struggle and suffering would again come as Jerusalem,(the city of David) would be destroyed by enemies. This whole process of history should be seen as an invitation to properly understand not just the struggles of God's chosen people but also the human condition. So often we (the religious part of humanity) want to proudly say, "We just need to have more faith, we must simply press on, enduring the storms, defiantly pressing our frustrated faces into the whipping winds of these discontented times, never questioning what we have been told, being defiant with questions of conscience or simply not allowing struggles to surface" but in this egocentric outlook we miss an alternative view. It is not only we who remain faithful to God but it is He who remains faithful to us in spite of our human condition. This is the miracle, similar to the miracle of healing, which brings home His invitation to, "Rest in Him." It brings about what I believe would seem to some an odd conclusion, it's not about saving the world, it's not about **earning** a place in heaven, it's not about achieving perfect righteousness but rather it's about letting ourselves be changed (it's about the prodigal son/ daughter coming home) and healed by the grace of God so that we can finally experience a gravitational pull which does not give way to distraction. It is about realizing that as we have been busy trying to manufacture a successful life (working away at finding ever new ways to draw water from a well) we have missed something or have been unaware of the loving watchful eye of God. Some type of suffering will often allow us to become aware of His presence and (as we turn toward Him) our eye can finally meet His eye and at that moment our world can change. I am not advocating that people need to be walking around engaged in meaningful debates of conscience 24/7 (this would be an anxious existence) but I do want to draw our attention to the way in which we sometimes learn to squelch or bury or tamp down meaningful questions which if answered can give a depth to our faith which nurtures an ever renewing sense of growth. If there is a devil's advocate this is what he wants to stop. This ever renewing sense of growth reflects a **process** of transformation which is primarily expressed through a willingness to feel the influence of a divine center and this influence can usher us into the awareness of the third dynamic of recovery.

Dynamic Three – Complexity vs Simplicity

The third dynamic is when a person in recovery allows what seems to be an ever increasing complex world to prevent them from embracing the simplicity of the path that is being laid before them.

> *The mind that is governed by the flesh is death but the mind that is governed by the Spirit is Life and Peace.*
> Rom 8:6

It goes without saying that whenever the word "flesh" is used (especially in our modern times) it triggers a kind of thought process that sees the mind being governed by the physical senses (sexuality) in a dominant or coercive way. The point that I would like to make is that in thinking about the mind being governed by the flesh we should also be open to thinking about a mind that is governed by reason alone. The exercise of the mind involves the use of reason but our reason can either be governed by the flesh (characterized by hostility toward God) in isolation or by the realm of the Spirit in the company of our Father *(Abba)* Rom 8:15. It is a secondary observation that in as much as we consciously think that our minds are being governed by reason modern research would also seem to indicate that we are often being guided by unconscious

desires and genetic predispositions. Paul himself states, "We know that the law is spiritual but I am unspiritual, sold as a slave to sin." Rom 7:14. In this context Paul is trying to explain the dynamic relationship between the Law and sin...how in some ways the Law is necessary for us to be able to recognize sin...but yet this recognition (in an ironic way) seems to at times draw us toward the sin itself. The underlying cause of sin is often a complicated matter but what seems more important is the awareness that our reason is not alone, as if some sort of solitary ruler of our lives, but acts in the company of other forces and realms.

The conflict or confrontation with *meaning* that we noted in dynamic two is expanded and reinforced by one's perceived awareness of the complexity of the world in which they live. It is not only that something has gone wrong in their own life but that they have a larger awareness that notices the disparity in things like wealth, education and a general concern or caring for others. In other words the harshness of the world overshadows the awareness of and importance of one human being reaching out to another with love. This quiet discontentment can eat away at them (us) in silence because they see no way out. I have often heard people in recovery describe this feeling as some sort of void or emptiness not only within themselves but also without. This void originates from a perceived lack of meaning or fullness in their daily lives. (They are a mouse on a wheel working for the man...they return to the grind day after day) In addition, they are overwhelmed or irritated by a world which seems to be constantly increasing in complexity. The inner workings of much of the technological devices they depend on is completely beyond their grasp and understanding things like globalization and world economics is like chasing some sort of "whisp-o-wil".

"For in much wisdom is much vexation and he who increases knowledge increases sorrow" Eccl 1: 18

"Our words are a blustering wind…we were born only yesterday and know nothing and our days on earth are but a shadow" Job 8: 2,9.

It is no longer amazing to "the discontented" that in today's modern society, all our science, all our efficiency, all our "advancement" has gotten us no closer to understanding our relationship to the big picture or to what some would call Truth. The argument could even be made that the more complex our society (and our thinking) becomes the more elusive are the answers. For those that are interested in answers to questions involving the meaning and purpose of their life or existence, frustration can rise up as their lone companion.

"So I hated life, because what is done under the sun was grievous to me; for all is vanity and a striving after wind." Eccl 2: 17

This is the outlook that exemplifies a mind governed by reason in the absence of Spirit. At the beginning of recovery, many of those who suffer are far from realizing that the source of their anxiety is the way in which their desire for God has been frustrated or thwarted by the way they choose or have somehow come to view the world.

In a book called "Addiction and Grace" Gerald May, M.D, states, *"After twenty years of listening to the yearnings of people's hearts, I am convinced that all human beings have an inborn desire for God. Whether we are consciously religious or not, this desire is our deepest longing and our most precious treasure. It gives us meaning. Regardless of how we describe it, it is a longing for love. It is a hunger to love, to* be loved, and to move closer to the Source of love. *This yearning is the essence of the human spirit; it is the origin of our highest hopes and most noble dreams.*"[15]

> "But something gets in the way. The longing at the center of our hearts repeatedly disappears from our awareness, and its energy is usurped by forces that are not at all loving. Our desires are captured and we give ourselves over to things that, in our deepest honesty we really do not want."[16] (this is something that recovering alcoholics can easily relate to but for non addicts or those well into successful recovery it can be more challenging to identify more subtle desires within us that "we really do not want")

I myself have at times experienced great confusion because of the vast amount of information that is available to almost anyone who knows how to click a mouse. If we want to defend this or that side of an argument we just need to keep clicking.

So we ask and sometimes even cry out (in prayer),

How do we find the "clearing" in the woods?

How do we find contentment and peace?

My conclusion is that we return to the simplicity of witnessing and experiencing the application of grace through the spirit. This is why we go to recovery meetings, so that we can experience and witness the healing nature of grace which always seems to be welcomed by a tolerant, caring and honest atmosphere. It goes without saying that all meetings do not bring about a grace filled experience but by encouraging and cultivating the honest sharing of one's struggles we can help create an atmosphere which is conducive to or welcomes grace. There is often a part of us that questions our experiences of grace because we prefer to have something to put our finger on, something we can put under a lens, where we can say, "Here, this is God". But yet we also can at times feel our inner world (cosmos) change as our mood or disposition transforms from being downcast to joyful. Once we begin to experience the healing nature of grace we can also begin to become aware of our own divine center. When we begin to live from this divine center we can begin to experience a life that knows simplicity.

In his book "Out of Solitude", Henri Nouwen talks about the idea of Cure vs Care in modernity. His main point is that a great deal of priority has and is being placed on cure (as in the case of pharmaceutical companies) and this is being done at the expense of care. He points out,

> *"By the honest recognition and confession of our human sameness we can participate in the care of God who came not to the powerful but to the powerless, not to be different but to be the same, not to take our pain away but to share it. Through this participation we can open our hearts to each other and form a new community."*[17]

Caring represents a movement, away from our self and towards others in community. Millions of recovery meetings take place every day and people from every walk of life sit down at the same type of healing table because they care about helping others recover and in so doing they end up caring for them self.

Why? One way to see this movement is to see how Recovery groups encourage us not to look for some kind of immediate cure of our problem but to realize how caring for our self involves caring for others and that any kind of cure we experience is dependent on this caring. There can be part of us; although, that cries out for cure and it is from this position of frustration that we ask, "How in the world does my hectic crazy mixed up life have anything to do with simplicity?.. and then we are reminded of the movement. We allow ourselves to see the inflow of grace, as *"Hope does not put us to shame, because God's love has been poured into our hearts through the Holy Spirit.* Rom 5:5. We allow ourselves to notice the way it makes us feel, the way it changes us, the way it transforms us...the way it flows out of us...we see the way it can change others in an instant as well as over time...and most of all we see that it is not intrinsically us but rather that which chooses to move through us, to nurture us, to love us, to sustain us. There is nothing more... simple.

Furthermore; as I understand it, simplicity is freedom... freedom from our addiction...and freedom from all the other stuff that society tells us we must have...to have value. Our inner universe which consists of all sorts of meaningful things (metaphorical planets or stars) that we have attached great emotional value to is no longer just some sort of chaotic whirlwind or void but rather something whose orbits are now held in balance by a gravitational source which is far greater than our self alone.

Our autonomy and independence often rise up to reinforce a skeptical view of seeing our inner world/cosmos as being held in balance by anything that is not in our control but this modern tendency can be addressed by learning to be open to more than one perspective. As an example if we use our imagination to catapult ourselves into outer space we would see not just how tiny we are in comparison to the rest of the universe but also how the structure of galaxies and planetary systems are somehow held together by what appears to be empty space. If we were then able to shrink ourselves to the size of a molecule or atom and hang out within our own body we would most likely see a familiar scene as electrons and protons would be revolving around the nucleus of a particular molecule. We might consider that an individual atom is nothing by itself, that it has nothing at all in common with the complicated and technologically advanced human being of today. It does appear odd, unless one begins to think about what could be the solitary life of an atom[viii], a group of electrons that tend to orbit one nucleus which has the ability to change, the ability to give away and take back parts of its self. Nowhere it would seem is an atom ever really alone, it is in constant contact with others around it and even if it were isolated by the use of some cruel mechanical device it would still be connected to the source of its creation. Individuals spend their entire life trying to find that thing or vocation about which they revolve; individuals wonder if they will ever find an orbit in which they will truly be at home, they wonder whether or not they or anybody else will ever come close to understanding the gravity of their existence. So perhaps it is fitting that in some ways a human life does in fact mirror the structure of an atom! It is these tiny planetary/universal structures that indeed make up our ensouled bodies/embodied souls. Now it goes without saying that there is not one central physical molecule or planet within a person's body but by being open to different perspectives we can easily see the reality (metaphorical validity) or need of things to be held in balance by some sort of gravitational force that is not us. The journey of identifying this force as a (our) divine center involves the admission that in as much as the complexity of the modern world is not an illusion so too is our capacity to see beyond ourselves not an illusion.

"For the creation was **subjected to frustration**, not by its own choice, but by the will of the one who subjected it, in the hope that the creation itself will be liberated from its bondage to decay and brought into the freedom and glory of the children of God." Rom 8:20-21

My task is not to here address the formal discipline of Spiritual Simplicity or to formally argue for the existence of a divine center (which I obviously believe in) but rather to draw our attention to a different point of view or prospective from which to live our

---

[viii] Please see appendix for more information on the ownership of atoms.

lives and the clear advantages it entails. When we consider living from a divine center, in one way or another, we are "seeking first the kingdom of God" and when we are doing this we are allowing God to influence our decision making. We are now more apt to experience freedom from anxiety (inner simplicity) because we receive what we have as a gift from God, we trust that He is caring for us and we are in a better position to offer what we have to others. . "*Can any one of you by worrying add a single hour to your life.*" Matt 6: 27. Our outward simplicity can also change as we review the way we value or accept the standards and values of our culture and society. All of this is easier said than done especially when one takes into consideration the power of our minds as they insist on running the show in isolation, without the loving guidance of a divine center and therefore in the absence of the realm of the Spirit.

> "*Some of us have tried to hold on to our old ideas and the result was nil until we let go absolutely. Remember that we deal with alcohol, cunning, baffling, powerful without help it is too much for us, but there is one that has all power, that one is God may you find him now. Half measures availed us nothing, we stood at the turning point, we asked his protection and care with complete abandon.*"[18] (*Alcoholics Anonymous, How it Works, 3rd ed, AA World Services*).

For me Alcoholics Anonymous represents a recovery organization of immense value and wisdom. It was one of the first places that I discovered grace in action and for that I will be forever grateful. But as we move forward into modernity we are witnessing a plethora of "12 – step" groups in what seems like every different shape and form. In some respects it is wonderful that recovery is available to all but in other respects it is unfortunate because the Spiritual aspect is either not allowed (for any number of reasons) or is simply deemed of no use. It is therefore important to say that there are Christian based recovery organizations[ix] that are available for those who sense a connection with a power greater than themselves and that responding to this connection or call is one of the best decisions that a person can make especially if they want to experience what true freedom can be.

[ix] Please explore "Celebrate Recovery.com" or "12 Steps with Christ.com"... or check out becoming involved in your local church community as a recovery advocate.

Man as Microcosm

My preference for the use of the "inner cosmos" metaphor is grounded in my independent study of John Calvin and The Institutes of Christian Religion. When I first read Book 1, chapter 5 I was struck by not only the way in which Calvin was giving direct attention to the average man but also the way in which philosophy was actually being complimented by a theologian.

> *"In attestation of his wondrous wisdom, both the heavens and the earth present us with innumerable proofs which force themselves on the notice of the most illiterate peasant who cannot open his eyes without beholding them. No man, however, though he be ignorant of these, is incapacitated for discerning such proofs of creative wisdom as may well cause him to break forth in admiration of the Creator. To investigate the motions of the heavenly bodies, to determine their positions, measure their distances, and ascertain their properties, demands skill, and a more careful examination; and where these are so employed, as the providence of God is there more fully unfolded, so it is reasonable to suppose that the mind takes a loftier flight, and obtains brighter views of his glory. The same is true in regard to the structure*

> *of the human frame. To determine the connection of
> its parts, its symmetry and beauty, with the skill of
> a doctor requires singular acuteness and yet all men
> acknowledge that the human body bears on its face
> such proofs of ingenious contrivance as are sufficient
> to proclaim the admirable wisdom of its Maker. Hence
> certain of the philosophers have not improperly called
> man a microcosm (miniature world), as being a rare
> specimen of divine power, wisdom and goodness, and
> containing with himself wonders sufficient to occupy
> our minds, if we are willing so to employ them.*[19]

Calvin continues on by stating that we all *"have in our own persons a factory where innumerable operations of God are carried on...but instead of bursting forth with praise we are more often inflated and swelled with pride. They feel how wonderfully God is working in them...and yet they inwardly suppress these feelings... They have no occasion to go farther than themselves by appropriating as their own that which has been given them from heaven."*[20]

My area of concern here is that we realize the importance of seeing the ready application of Calvin's concern to our modern time. I believe that Calvin saw the power of this metaphor and even more directly saw how its incorrect use (by those with a preference for philosophical outlooks) would lead to the placement of our self at the center of who we are instead of God.

This is not just a problem of those who suffer from addiction but it is a problem that is more easily seen because of the way it is magnified in the actions of an addict. When we allow our inner world, our thoughts, our dreams, our concerns, our weaknesses and our courage or lack there of... to rotate only about our self and our need (or worse yet don't spend time in reflection at all) we become the prey of the patterns of this world. Calvin saw this threat as being reinforced by what he calls, "the philosopher outlook." The principle problem that he sees with this outlook is its tendency to overlook the corruption of nature or the brokenness of man. Calvin takes special care to differentiate the Christian position from the philosophical position of the Stoics. *"For we do not with the Stoics imagine a necessity consisting of a perpetual chain of causes, and a kind of involved series contained in nature, but we hold that God is the disposer and ruler of all things."*[21] Now this does; of course, carry with it philosophical implications but I would like to at least attempt to narrow our focus to realize specifically how a quality discussion of *man as microcosm* can indeed be used to not only be of use in identifying three dynamics of recovery but also to combat the philosophical outlook of Stoicism and consequently its modern expressions in humanism and privatized spirituality.

During the birth of Christianity one of the chief philosophical schools was Skepticism and in many ways Stoicism rose up in response by championing the ability of the individual to have courage to "take fate and death upon oneself" or in other words affirm the value of self (self – affirmation) by recognizing their own power of being. The Stoic had a personal and social courage that was a real alternative to Christian courage. But the victory of the Christian Church pushed Stoicism into an obscurity from which it would only emerge in the beginning of modern times. To see the way in which Stoicism appeals to modernity I believe it is easiest to look at it from three different aspects as it relates to Christianity. These are a) its sense of mystery b) its more technical or process elements and c) what it seems to lack. In summary I will close with comments on emotion and tribalism as these have been and continue to be threads of interest which can be rightfully used as a lens through which to see the impact that an individual's mindset (how they define their relation to God and others, especially society as a whole) can have on their daily life

The Mystery

Stoicism champions' reason but there is also a mysterious element in this conception of reason that needs to be emphasized and held in contrast to a more modern conception of reason. In order to understand this we need to talk about "The Logos" (or **The Word** as it is referred to by Christians..John 1). Heraclitus (not a stoic) was the first philosopher to use this word and he saw it as the law that determines the movements of all reality. The Stoics define The Logos as the divine power that is present in everything that is. It has three aspects, the law of nature (the principal according to which all things move, the divine seed), the moral law (innate within us, Kant's practical reason as an example), and man's ability to recognize reality (theoretical reason). Salvation for the Stoic is reached through attaining wisdom through the execution of reason. The man who is determined by the Natural Law or the Logos is the wise man. *"But the stoics were not optimists, everybody does not become a wise man. Perhaps there are only a few who reach this ideal. All the others were either fools or stood somewhere between the wise and the foolish."*[22] So Stoicism held a basic pessimism or resignation about the majority of human beings.

Technical and Process elements

So now let's take a look at the process of self affirmation. According to Paul Tillich the most modern representative of a neo-stoicism is Spinoza. (He is generally described as a rationalist and considered alongside Descartes and Leibniz). *"In him as in nobody else the ontology of courage is elaborated. For Spinoza, as for the Stoics, the courage to be is not one thing beside others. It is an expression of the essential act of everything that participates in being, namely self-affirmation."*[23] We need to be aware that this is modern humanism… yes we are recognizing the power of being, a divinity that is within us and perhaps also without but we are doing it under our own power...under our own power of reason. Our striving toward self preservation and self affirmation makes a thing what it is. It is our power and the power of our action. So we identify our essence (being), and our power, and therefore are able to affirm our self. It is added that this affirmation should lead to the development of virtue. Virtue is the power of acting exclusively according to one's true nature. One's degree of virtue corresponds to the degree one is striving for and able to affirm his own being. *"But self affirmation is affirmation of one's essential being, and the knowledge of one's essential being is mediated through reason, the power of the soul (conscious mind) to have adequate ideas. Therefore to act unconditionally out of virtue is the same as to act under the guidance of reason, to affirm one's essential being or true nature."*[24] What this is really getting at is the necessary connection between reason and morality (Kant is one of the chief proponents of this point of view)). One way to look at the benefits of this outlook is to review the history of a Stoic Roman Emperor like Marcus Aurelius. The concept of The Logos was applied to the political situation. The meaning of the natural law was that every man and woman participates in reason by virtue of the fact that they were a human being. So women, children and slaves who were previously seen as inferior by old Roman Law became equalized under new Roman Law. It was not Christianity that did this but new Roman Emperors. Universal citizenship was given to every human being based on the fact that all at least had the potential to become educated (there of course is the sense of pessimism that a great deal will remain foolish but the idea that virtue is involved in decision making should be clear). Further benefits of this type of outlook are interesting and can be talked about in relation to anxiety and neurosis. One of the areas of emphasis for the Stoics is that courage stands against despair by taking anxiety into itself. They point out that when one is not able to do this anxiety in essence wins the battle and escapes and develops into neurosis. Hence we have the beginning of psychological therapy. An underlying theme here is that anxiety is completely different than fear in that fear has a biological purpose whereas anxiety is biologically useless because it has no identifiable object.

What Stoicism lacks

Stoicism could have never become Christianity because Christianity could not assimilate the genuine Stoic attitude. Stoicism accepts the attitude of cosmic resignation while Christianity promotes faith in cosmic salvation. So in other words (some would say) Christianity provides a better solution to the human condition because of the individual character of the Savior Jesus Christ and the concrete historical basis of the Old Testament . Stoicism is although, a basic religious attitude because it is how people (some of whom were the noblest figures of antiquity) answered the problems of existence and conquered the anxieties of fate and death. The Stoic had a social and personal courage that was a real alternative to Christian courage. It is this use of courage (as noted above) that leads to self affirmation and has a direct parallel in Christianity (which competes with stoicism) of receiving salvation through grace. I guess I could just try and leave the subject here and simply say that grace makes the difference but things are just not that easy! Why? Because of the Logos. If we really dig in and see how Seneca (one of the chief architects of Stoicism) talks about things we find that reason is not just looked upon as limited cognitive function (calculating) but includes all mental functions (**the personal center**) *"Stoic courage presupposes the surrender of the personal center to the Logos of being, it is participation in the divine power of reason, transcending the realm of passions and anxieties. The courage to be is the courage to affirm our own rational nature, in spite of everything in us that conflicts with its union with the rational nature of being-itself."*[25] It may be of interest to note that Seneca was the first to say, "Nothing is terrible in things except fear itself." (I guess Roosevelt was a Stoic!). So my point is that the Stoic's use of reason has a deep sense of mystery and really does parallel the Christian experience of surrender and coming to faith but I believe to see them as interchangeable would be a costly mistake. For the Christian faith is not something that a person earns through the proper execution of reason under their own power rather faith is a gift and can be given and is given to some of the most uneducated people in the world because at its root it is grace and the gift of grace is the miracle that the death of Christ has made possible.

Another way to look at all of this is to try and think about the difference between the Power of Being and the Ground of Being. There surely is a necessary distinction between the two. Yes, each human being has within them the power of being but this is not the ground of being. My point would be that there is a necessary logical separation which takes place between the ground of being and the power of being and this gap or separation is fundamental to our existence and to think that it can be overcome by our own willpower is foolish but always tempting to explore! Why? Who doesn't want to be God?

Seneca says, *"that while God is **beyond** suffering the true stoic is **above** it. Suffering this implies, contradicts the nature of God. It is impossible for him to suffer, he is beyond it. The stoic as a human being is able to suffer, but he need not let suffering conquer the center of his rational being. He can keep himself above it as a consequence of that which is not his essential being but is accidental in him. The distinction between beyond and above implies a value judgment. The wise man who courageously conquers desire, suffering and anxiety surpasses God himself."*[26]

Personally, I believe that God can and does suffer...I have no explanation other than to say it is something that I deeply feel. In addition I believe that the Stoic has the courage to affirm himself in spite of faith and death but does not have the courage to affirm himself in spite of sin and guilt…one has to turn to the strength of Christianity to investigate the true depths of our personal center.

<u>Emotion</u>

Now, in turning to the topic of Emotion we can readily see the way in which Stoicism attracts the human personality. We all like calmness, at least in not wanting to see the extremes of almost any emotion for extended periods of time and it goes without saying that anytime we can get reasons for why we shouldn't get caught up in the misfortunes of others and let them affect our overall outlook on life they are appreciated and perhaps assimilated into the perhaps mistaken frame through which we watch the world.

> *"The most beautiful thing that we can experience is the mysterious. It is the source of all true art and **science**. He to whom this "emotion" is a stranger, who can no longer pause to wonder, or stand rapt in awe, is as good as dead. His eyes are closed." Albert Einstein*

Reason alone is not sufficient in decision making as room needs to be made for faith. What seems often hard to explain is how this use of faith expresses itself in daily life or in other words the mechanics of faith in decision making associated with emotions. This is a tall order because emotions seem to happen in an instant, they are not so much produced by reason as they are reacted/responded to with reason…the mission always seems to be to tame the beast or condition oneself to react/respond to emotion in a slow and methodical way…and at times we fail, and this is especially the case for those struggling with addiction as well as anger management issues. Emotion can present itself as an instant physical reaction to news reports or photographs or to real time things happening to those closest to us etc…so reason which involves conscious thought seems to be always secondary. What does this mean? I would respond that emotion and reason are often simultaneous, our minds are reasonably processing what we see or hear and direct (sometimes unconsciously) the physical response of emotion in its various and hopefully appropriate forms depending on our previous experience. Today, I would use these ideas to support the thought that emotion cannot be given a secondary position in relation to reason because it is impossible but rather the goal is to see them as two equal forces within the individual that need to be brought into balance.

> "A fifth element was added to the Platonic tradition which came from Aristotle. The divine is a form without matter, perfect in itself. This is the profoundest idea in Aristotle. The highest form called, 'God', is moving the world, not causally by pushing it from the outside, but by driving everything finite toward him by means of love. In spite of his apparent scientific attitude toward reality, Aristotle developed one of the greatest systems of love. He said that God, the highest form, or pure actuality, as he called it, moves everything by being loved by everything. Everything has the desire to unite itself with the highest form, to get rid of the lower forms in which it lives, where it is in the bondage of matter. (brings to mind living in world but not being of it) Later the Aristotelian God, as the highest form, entered into Christian theology and exerted a tremendous influence upon it."[27]

What's the point? My point would be that the source of emotion as well as reason is love (the divine form). This being the case, we can see that the proper course of action is not to dominate emotion with reason but rather to bring the two into balance as they both can be brought into balance by the action of the highest divine form (grace). What we see here is a continued emphasis on the necessary incompleteness of individual (the inability of a person to achieve perfection under their own power) in the absence of their connection to the highest form. It is the realization of the gravitational pull of God that can do wonders for the person that is struggling with emotional balance but it always takes place in the learning experience of a person's lifetime. The process is never absolutely complete or in other words there is always another way to see one more of the infinite faces of God. I guess it is a bit much to say that emotional balance is about seeing the face of God but I do believe that when a person is troubled (for instance a person early on in recovery) and experiences a sense of healing by speaking and listening to others who have a common awareness of brokenness it definitely is a way of experiencing the presence of God.

Tribalism

If we are going to apply the concept of the inner cosmos and its implied warning against the modern expressions of Stoicism then talking about the concept of tribalism is needed or at least one way to see how modern scientific outlook needs to be counterbalanced by an awareness of an ongoing dialogue which always keeps a door open to the grace of God.

E O Wilson, in his book, "The Social Conquest of Earth", suggests that **healthy** tribalism is the way that the world or society has been formed to date and that in order for success to continue the healthy aspects of tribalism need to be realized in a way which allows them to flourish but unfortunately this may be something that will present us with the greatest of challenges.. On some levels this seems fine to me in that different groups should be allowed to exist as long as they are tolerant of other groups and at least open to having interaction and the ability to assimilate others into their tribe when possible. In a basic way it seems to be a kind of "live and let live" mentality which provides for continual progress and is built at times on necessary self sacrifice for the greater good.

From a pragmatic scientific position I do not believe that I would argue with this outlook. But I got the idea that there might be a way to use our discussion of Stoicism and the way in which it is seen as developing into modern humanism as a backdrop against which we could see at the very least the benefits of looking at things from a alternative perspective.

"The background to all these controversies was what Tillich called the eternal dialogue that continues in history between Plato and Aristotle. It is the dialogue between a philosophy of wisdom and a philosophy of science or as Tillich puts it between the ontological and the cosmological approaches to God."[28] (the ontological approach is seen as platonic and more theological while the cosmological approach is Aristotelian and utilizes science, the structure of the cosmos, as a way towards supporting belief...the latter lends itself more to the development of modern humanism which gives science priority over God.)

Now clearly this is pretty complex stuff and because I really do not want to delve too into endless philosophical discussion I am going to try and quickly present what I think the alternative perspective could be. So we have two different viewpoints. The one approach (Platonic) is concerned with the depths of life through the attainment of wisdom in all its forms. The other approach started out as an approach toward the divine but its concentration on the priority of science began to limit its investigation of the world to only that which was clearly and distinctly present on the surface of things (utilizing the scientific method). The former approach did not accept this limitation and freely explored the depths however obscure they seem to the scientist. The key for me lies in the observation that although these two approaches may seem like opposites, I think that they are also necessarily opposite ends of the same continuum. The point would be that in order for us to have a complete system one approach does not have to overcome the other and prove its dominance but rather they need and can even serve one another for instance with inspiration and new discoveries of facts...this dual approach values the dialogue... values the entire arc of history and recognizes the necessity and value of each approach in that in the absence of one the system is no longer a system. This is where the danger lies (in insisting that one side of things reign supreme).

So if we take this alternative perspective of "an ongoing dialogue" and apply it to the issue of tribalism in relation to Stoicism, humanism and Christianity what do we find? My reflection has lead me to the conclusion that if tribalism is looked upon as the default position of man (which I do not argue) it suffers from three primary complications a) morality b)individual meaning and purpose and c) complexity of tribe identification (especially in modernity).

The exact process of the development of **morality** can be argued but it would seem that all tribes develop some sense of morality dependent upon their experience. This sense of morality often causes tension or judgment between tribes. If my life and experience has taught me anything it has taught me that at some level all human beings have an inborn desire for God or at least to know the **meaning and purpose** for their life. It should be quite apparent that the existence of tribes begins to answer this question at the surface level of a person's life. "*I belong to this group and they have my allegiance. This gives me purpose.*" But many people get to a point in their life when the group or **tribe mentality is found wanting**. Sometimes this can be because of education and at other times it can result from some type of traumatic experience which causes them to question fundamental assertions of the group. The individual cries out for something more...this feeling can be answered by a personal relationship with God (Ground and power of being). The Stoics addressed the feeling by learning how to take the anxiety of fate and death into themselves through the exercise of the courage of self affirmation, with an eye towards the entire personal center (something in addition to the calculating mind – total reason). One way to look at this would be to see how this turbulence within tribes fosters the development of new tribes or at least different organizations within tribes which seems to work against unity. Successful tribes would be the ones that are capable of incorporating various viewpoints or those that have an eye for the type of unity that can be found through allowing the presence of diversity.

The other thing that strikes me about tribalism is the difficulty in establishing the criteria that a group must meet to qualify as a tribe. It is relatively easy to say that we just have to realize that this or that group is a tribe especially when we are looking at something in history but in real time can we say that heterosexuals are a tribe, what about conservative vs liberal heterosexuals, what about conservative vs liberal people who choose to live in alternative lifestyles?, should all people who are comfortable with racism be a tribe? Is big business a tribe? Can there be tribes within tribes? But wait a minute doesn't that mean that in the last analysis we are just one big tribe anyway? It can get confusing (**and complex**) fast but if we stay grounded and just say that in general the tribal structure is the default tool of how humanity has progressed we can realize that the challenge is not in coming up with a new structure (for after all tribalism, as an analysis of experience has taught us… is the default) but rather in seeing how we need to work within the tribal structure to address how continued progress can be made. My conclusion is that it is not about the "live and let live" mentality but rather about being ready and able to work in the media of life, on the surface as well as in the depths… regardless of what tribe to which one belongs. There can be Unity in Diversity and this unity can readily be seen as a gateway to seeing the structure of the Trinity as an appropriate metaphor to guide our tribal existence... distinct and necessary difference but yet unity and sameness and an outpouring of love.

Our freedom is found in our ability to make good choices, as we control or keep our emotions in check (balance), but we should not make the mistake of thinking that our emotions are not one of or the key thing that motivates us to make those very choices. The whole dialogue thing between Plato and Aristotle (which continues today) really struck me in that it really does seem to reflect the truth of things...it is the dialogue between emotion and reason that results in action. In as much as the dialogue continues to take place between humanism and Christianity it is also taking place within each one of us...the task is to not see the dialogue as useless, to not let one engulf the other...to not let one fool the other into thinking that they themselves are somehow God or are well enough on their own to do without Him. Some time ago I stumbled upon a book, at a book sale up north, called "Descartes Error". It was written by Antonio R Damasio, M.D., Ph.D., head of the department of neurology at Iowa University. This is another over simplification but here we have a scientist working at the neurological level of the brain in coordination with living subjects who have unfortunately received profound brain injuries due to accidents etc...One of his primary findings was that if an area of the brain that produces emotion is damaged it can sometimes move to a different area of the brain and secondarily that in the absence of an area of the brain producing emotion the rational areas of the brain lack the motivation to act. I just wanted to note this result as a way to support the interdependence of emotion and reason and I hope that the notion of being able to see this interplay within our self as well as in society (the tribal landscape) can bring about the type of outlook that appreciates where Stoicism falls short (*because of an attitude of resignation about the masses, a lack of a personal relationship with God, and an elevation of reason to a position of priority over emotion which can bring about equality with God*) and Christianity excels.

In conclusion Paul Tillich died in the late 1960"s and one of his closest friends was another well known philosopher, Martin Buber. Tillich was a protestant while Buber was a Jew therefore they were from different "tribes" but they were able to be the closest of friends because they believed in (while being comfortable in their own distinct religions) a type of universalism that recognized, "The God above the God of religion." This concept is indeed a controversial idea but if it is an idea that allows people of different faiths to sit down at the same table to have a dialogue than it has its value. It may seem a bit weird at first but if we reflect on the concept of the Logos (its age and the truth it represents) then it may become possible to recognize the truth that all religions hold in common and this is the truth that invites us to not just hear the echoes of the past but to generate an active dialogue into the future where we work with the surface of things just as much as we work with the depths.

A Spiritual Exercise of Mind

I often have searched for ways to support or reinforce a discussion of Spirituality and one of the best ways I have come up with it to utilize the most basic symbol of all...the circle. (It is usually used as a symbol for wholeness and unity but it can also be used in much more basic ways). When a person gets up in the morning or begins there day they have certain things that they must attend to. They have to reach over and try to turn off the alarm clock, we can view this as the first circle of the day, then one must get up and take care of their immediate needs such as brushing teeth etc, this can be looked upon as another circle, then the person has to address needs of family interaction, another circle, and then the person has to address work relations, another circle, and then a person might look at addressing their relation to the larger world around them through social media, another circle. So in a simplistic or down to earth way it can be seen that a person's daily life is the management of a certain number of circles. The exercise that I sometimes find helpful is to imagine that a group of average members of society (a cross section of cultures etc...) has somehow been randomly selected and then divided into two groups so that they can take part in a spiritual experiment of sorts. One of these groups has at least one person struggling with addiction. They find themselves positioned in front of a large flat surface, a large oak table or perhaps a granite stone, the smooth surface has a way of attracting attention, it invites some sort of interaction with it, the sliding of a hand along its surface or the admiration of the seeming depth of the grain or stone. The invitation comes, they are asked by a polite computer screen to lay out their circles upon this surface, some individuals are meticulous, they work very hard at trying to predict what the study is actually studying and therefore take great care in the way they organize their circles because after all someone is watching!, it can take hours...and then the time comes for the analysis...they are to asked to judge their own performance... how have they arranged the circles?...which ones have they given priority?...do some overlap with others? Is there one that is rising up in comparison to the others?...have one or more been put off to the side so that they can never come in contact with the others? Are all the circles present or do some remain hidden? Judging their own performance was something that the participants in group one were not expecting, again it takes some of them hours to complete the survey questions. And then we turn our attention to group number two which consists of at least one individual that is suffering from some kind of addiction. He immediately draws our attention...there he is standing before the large flat surface looking up at the cold flat computer screen which is issuing instructions... he mutters quietly to himself, "put my circles where? What a bunch of nonsense!" Nevertheless he reaches for his circles and tosses them out onto the surface, there they bounce and interact and some fall from the table, he is too tired to bother picking them up. The only reason that he was there in the first place was because of the poster that said he would be paid $25.00 to take part in a study. He also knew or at least suspected that the only reason he was selected for the study was because he admitted that he was struggling with addiction. He knew he was being watched, he felt he was being judged. As he watched his circles slide across the large flat surface there was a real lack of focus...all the ideas, all the things he wanted to do almost never seemed to come together…they never seemed to balance out. He stood there before the table, looking down and then up at the screen. He asked, "Is the test over, can I go now?" There was no answer. He was very tired but in the silence he did begin to feel a sense of guilt, he bent down and picked up the two circles that had dropped off the table. He recognized one that he had long forgotten, he held it for a moment in admiration and felt a sense of longing, he then gently placed it in the center of the table, nudging some of the other circles aside and then looked up at the screen once again and said, "I'm done, finished." He completed the survey, retrieved his circles and left.

In making a comparison between the two groups there is certainly two different situations here, often there is a certain kind of sadness felt for the disgruntled man or worse yet a kind of negative judgment, a looking down upon, "why doesn't he just get his act together?" Upon closer examination; although, I think there is a kind of truth to be found here in the discontentment of the man from group two. He recognizes the exercise as not being reflective of his life. In the follow up interview he is asked what would it take to make it more accurate. He looks at the questioner and sarcastically says, "Dude, there is no table, there is no weird surface…the circles of my life have no place to be at rest, they are just spinning out in space." The truth that is found here rightly suggests that the large flat surface only has a limited use in this exercise. Its only role is to provide a place where the circles can be arranged and hopefully in some way understood but the real test comes when the surface is removed or suddenly vanishes. What happens then is truly amazing, we begin to see an accurate picture or symbol for a healthy life. Our inner cosmos, hopefully in balance, floats there and free before our very eyes. The circles of our lives are like orbits, some of them attract enough attention that they even form planets but even these planets need a center about which to revolve, something that they are drawn to, a gravitational pull which keeps them in balance. *"Each of us has within us undoubted evidence of the heavenly grace by which we live, move and have our being."* (Acts 17:28) The challenge is to bring what seem like separate circles or orbits together into a structure that works. It is not just about marveling at things going on in nature around us but also about marveling at things going on within us and it all starts when we begin to operate from a divine center. It is in this acknowledgment of the depth of our being where our experience of the mystery and miracle of life can find its rightful home.

Conclusion

I believe that at times we all like to think that there are areas or projects of our lives that are complete or finished. By stressing what I see as the dynamic components of recovery and the roots of wisdom (scripture) from which they come and the resistance that everyday life presents, I have attempted to bring home the idea that when it comes to cultivating a relationship with God that we are always and forever, "on the way". When we embrace this perspective it helps to combat against not only complacency in Christian recovery but also the Christian walk of life. Our modern times seem to have brought with them an evolving sense of "disenchantment" with organized religion. I do not want to suggest that this is not the case but I do want to emphasize that throughout history man has often championed reason at the expense of religion and in many ways we are obviously seeing this trend continue with the rise of secularity and the dominance of humanistic psychology/ philosophy. When I think about the person in recovery or the person struggling with religion in modernity I always see a person who has at least taken the time to step back at look at the world in which they live and they have come to the valid conclusion that something has gone terribly wrong. The way to which we respond to this sense of wrongness is of great importance. Do we drink or use ourselves into oblivion? Do we allow negativity to influence the way we relate to others or do we realize that in a sense we have been invited to become conscious of ourselves and the world around us in a way which can bring us freedom, love and peace. We can and do recognize a part of ourselves (in our inner being) that has always wanted to do what is right (to follow God) and yet another part of ourselves that pulls us toward something else, to look down on ourselves, to look down on others, to despair in the world. There are ways that the world does indeed make us a kind of prisoner as we come into it facing readymade and sometimes questionable expectations of achievement or success. But yet some of us are aware of a kind of backdrop or veil behind it all which however illusive it may seem is undeniable. It may not call to us but it does affect us, it does make its presence known, it always has…

I am convinced that in one way or another we are all called by the mystery and miracle of life. As we search for meaning and purpose we select different frames through which to see and interpret this world. We also can at times realize that many things are competing for our attention. How do we choose rightly? How do we incorporate the will of God into our decision making? The truth of the matter is that the answers are not always clear. We may at one time or another find our self in a situation in which we truly cannot understand how it reflects a world in which God is deeply involved. Our task; therefore, is not to insist on our reason to provide the answers but to come to the realization that as a child of God we are far more that a just a "thinking and doing" being. It is as if we have stumbled upon a radical idea that stands at the edge of reason and has the courage to cry out to something equally real. There is a part of me that even now immediately asks the question, "Well, if I am not thinking or doing something what else is there?" Today, in as much as I still hear myself asking this question, I also hear it being answered but the difference is that the answer that I hear comes from the depths of who I am and reminds me that I am so much more than a thinking mind. It is difficult to live from a part of ourselves that we cannot know in a reasonable way... then again perhaps it is easy for some but it would not be those people to whom this book has been directed.

In one of Sorren Kierkegaard's most famous essays, "Fear and Trembling" he does an in depth examination of faith and because he writes the essay through the eyes of someone else, "Johannes de Silentio", it creates the question as to whether Kierkegaard truly feels what he is writing or if he is trying to capture the feelings of someone else like perhaps the average man or woman. As the essay unfolds he examines faith from different perspectives and at one point uses an interesting metaphor. He states, *"I can swim in life, but for this mysterious floating (true faith) I am too heavy."*[29] My question is when we look out at the world today does this not seem to be the more popular position? When we look deeply into our own hearts can we really not make the same statement or does our heart confirm a certain sense of doubt? The genius of Kierkegaard is that he sees this window into our heart and he wants us to see it as well so that we not only can give up our grip on the world (and its grip on us) but also that we realize the immensity of what we receive through faith. There is nothing for us to reach out and grasp but there is everything for us to humbly stand and receive.

It is a paradox that our relationship with God is an activity that requires our attention as something that is always "on the way" but yet faith is something that we can't earn but rather is a gift. By viewing Christian Recovery as the dynamic process that allows us to examine and confront the tension of everyday life we can slowly learn that in as much as it is important to learn how to swim (to learn to love God, ourselves and our neighbors) it is also possible for us to float as we take in the breath of God and breathe out a life worth living.

It is of critical importance that people who struggle with drug and alcohol addiction become aware that they can indeed find their way back to sobriety but I think that a message which is equally important is that they (we) can also find their way home. This home is found in the company of our Father (Abba) and it is built on the foundation of the gift of faith.

Lord have mercy upon our tired souls, that we may know your presence always.

God Bless.

Appendix – The Ownership of Atoms

The ice was already off of the lake but it was far from being alive, at least not in the way that it would be in the coming summer months. Winter had given way to spring. Peace and quiet revealed the true nature of this crystal clear pool of water that seemed to be calmly surrendering to the sound of the wind whispering through the trees. I found a resting spot on the end of an overturned rowboat and was pleasantly surprised by a cool breeze. My attention was drawn to its presence and I began to wonder several things, what was its origin, of what was it made, and being that it is a thing which can be felt with the senses does it simply disappear when its momentum ends? I was curious as to whether or not there was any way that wisdom and knowledge could somehow be absorbed or passed on by such a thing as a breeze. Such a simple common every day event, why in the world should it invite such scrutiny? In the usual course of things knowledge is delivered by word of mouth or in the manner of books such as the Bible or Koran and of course all the many other books of history but it also seems to somehow sink into us as it is revealed in sudden moments of realization that everyone experiences in greater and lesser forms. It slowly became apparent that using the wind as much more than just a metaphor can sometimes be appropriate. It is a difficult topic for a technical world.

The modern mind is constantly being trained to trust that technology, and the overwhelming amount of information that it provides, is good and most of the time the facts that experience provides bear this out. This contributes to the formation of an attitude which values facts as opposed to opinions or unfounded ideas. When confronted with the idea that a breeze could be something more than a breeze, one maintaining the above attitude might be inclined to say, "Why in the world, someone can't stay grounded in reality and explain things like they actually are is beyond me?" This is a very important question and represents what I see as the modern outlook, which emphasizes looking at facts and making unbiased decisions based on the principles of the scientific method. For centuries belief in God was not even an option especially for those that feared and were taught from a young age about His punishing ways, there was no impetus or framework within which one could question their beliefs. Today our more "modern" culture is full of diversity, complexity and unfortunately anxiety all of which present the individual with what can seem like impossible choices especially in relation to religions, which are looked upon as something other than facts. The result seems obvious, we either don't make a choice and just float without being anchored anywhere or we accept without questioning or we question and are hopefully able to come to a place where we can allow our intellectual curiosity to find some sort of satisfaction or rest (we find a place where our anchor holds). It is; therefore, important that if a person is going to speak to the modern individual in a way which calls into question "the way that he or she thinks" one must do it in a manner which does not ignore the facts of science nor the benefits of a life based in and on faith.

That day on the lakeshore I was in a reflective mood and was open to the workings of nature around me and as always, part of myself was looking for anything special that could improve my outlook or mood. I wanted to see the breeze as a mysterious and miraculous thing but fortunately or not my intellectual side rose up in rebellion and made clear its opposition in response to the notion that the breeze was anything other than a breeze. Therefore, I went about my day taking care of the many things that for one reason or another needed to done but as luck would have it, my mind would often return to that refreshing feeling that almost any gentle breeze generates within, the natural reflex arc of breathing deep and receiving its presence as that which somehow enriched my entire being and then letting it go back out.

> "A person will suffocate if he or she just keeps breathing in. The Jewish name for the Holy One, literally unspeakable, is "Yahweh," which we now believe was an imitation of the sound of breathing in and breathing out. It could not be uttered but only breathed. The sacred name of God (Exodus 3:14) is already revealing the deepest pattern of all reality, which is **the cycle of taking in and giving back out**. It is the shape of all creation called a Trinitarian circle of indwelling and outpouring, and was the very shape of God and of all reality formed in God's image. It is all there, like a cosmic hidden code, at the very beginning and foundation of our Traditions."[30] Richard Rohr, *Breathing Under Water*.

So, in the days and months that followed a gentle debate began between the side of my intellect dedicated to my spiritual nature and the side of my intellect dedicated to reasoning. Questions were posed.

Of what is the breeze made?
The breeze is made of air.

Of what is air made?

Air is made of 78.09% nitrogen, 20.95% oxygen, .039% carbon dioxide, 2.0% water vapor.

The origin of the large percentage of oxygen in our atmosphere is a mystery; to this day its cause is unidentified. The movement of air is referred to as wind; a gentle wind is a breeze.

What is the cause of wind?

Wind is caused by the interaction of high and low pressure systems which on a very large scale form Jet Streams.

What are Jet Streams?

The actual appearance of jet streams result from the complex interaction between many variables - such as the location of high and low pressure systems, warm and cold air, and seasonal changes. They meander around the globe, dipping and rising in altitude/latitude, splitting at times and forming eddies, and even disappearing altogether to appear somewhere else. The origin or source of high and low pressure systems is found in movement of different masses of air which in turn is caused by their density or the number of **atoms** therein contained.

What are atoms?

Atoms are made up of protons, neutrons and electrons. Protons and neutrons combine to form the nucleus and the electrons form a cloud which essentially orbits the nucleus. Atoms reflect the basic building blocks of matter. They correspond to the elements in the periodic table.

What is the lifespan of an atom?

The lifespan of an atom is measured by what is called the "half-life." This is the time that it takes for half (50%) of a bunch of unstable atoms to decay. For carbon-14, this number is 5,730 years. For different radioactive atoms, this number can be anywhere from a tiny fraction of a second to minutes, hours, days, or even millions of years. But, in all these cases, the point of the decay is to reach a type of atom that is stable. Ultimately, even these stable atoms have a limit imposed by the lifetime of proton (>10^{25} years). The best estimate of the present age of the universe is the much smaller number of 10^{10} years, so for all practical purposes, atoms are forever.

With the above scientific knowledge we can make some conclusions. First, because the earth exist in a relatively (the sun remains a life giving source of energy) enclosed atmosphere the vast percentage of the atoms of matter that make up the periodic table stay within the confines of our planet and our atmosphere. Second, because atoms are for all intent and purposes immortal there is at least a small chance that the atoms which formed the winds of the earth thousands of years ago are some of the same atoms that form the winds of today. Third, the atoms that make up our bodies have the potential of being very old. We should also be aware that in certain chemical reactions atoms can be rearranged in order to form new compounds but the underlying premise remains, the basic elements of the atoms are in essence being recycled…as they pass through the process of transformation.

What does this mean?

It means of course that our atoms, the ones that makeup our unique body as well as the world around us are much older than we are ourselves. As any person sits and feels the body which they view as their own it is hard to consider that the atoms which construct it are not their own. It is odd to consider that we do not own our atoms. Science does not lie. Our atoms were around before our birth and therefore the proper conclusion is that we "lease" our atoms we do not "own" them. This conclusion brings about a much more important question. If our atoms are leased and were around before we were than what do we own? And better yet, who or what do we lease them from?

In order to answer these questions we must talk about what we call the soul. Just keep in mind that the atoms need something to cling to, need something around which to rally themselves, a purpose, a reason to collect themselves and begin the foundations of what is to become a human being. When we think about the physical development of a person in relation to the dawning of consciousness and the awareness of the soul, rarely is there any kind of talk about the correlation of the two. It seems necessarily so, that at some point in time there is a correlation between the number and kind of atoms an individual has and the appearance of some limited form of self awareness or some limited form of consciousness. It would also seem necessarily so that the specific number and kind of atoms being present precede the consciousness. Now surely a person's self awareness and their soul should not be equated and that is not what I am trying to suggest, rather I am trying to draw attention to the necessary existence of a certain kind of relationship between the body and soul. Matter (our bodies) may have a very logical purpose, to protect the soul, the grand soul (fabric of the universe) as well as our individual souls or what could be seen as our individual piece of the fabric of the universe. Clearly, providing some kind of proof of the necessary existence of the soul is beyond the scope and purpose of this small essay about the mystery and miracle of a cool breeze, but what I am offering is a way towards a positive viewpoint from which to make sense of it all. So, if we own anything we own a piece of the fabric of the universe, a gift freely given, to which our consciousness has been in some way attached. The real question therefore, is not who it came from but rather what do we do with it now that we have it?

"*It is something to be able to paint a particular picture,
or to carve a statue, and so to make a few objects
beautiful, but it is more glorious to carve and paint
the very atmosphere and medium through which we
look, which morally we can do. To affect the quality
of the day, that is the highest of arts. We are tasked
to make our lives, even in their details, worthy of the
contemplation of our most elevated and critical hour.*"
Journals, Henry David Thoreau.

We must always learn to look beyond just what is ours or just what we own, we can always ask more especially in terms of how we are connected to history or what we see as the past. So for instance, we can ask the question, if our atoms are much older than ourselves does their age carry with them any kind of benefit? Does an individual atom have the ability to carry with it any kind of memory or information or emotion? I find it somehow very comforting to entertain the notion that history is all about us, in its atomic form, it is all right here, right now, it's just been reformed and recycled but it has gone nowhere, it is all here within the confines of our planet and its atmosphere constantly being warmed and energized by the light of the sun. A simple walk down a city block or country road could involve countless encounters with ancient times. Every day we push ourselves about through a fog of atoms, whether we see it or not.

The cold reasoning presence of science answers clearly, " No" to all of the above questions. A single atom is not alive, it is an inanimate object, just as a rock is inanimate, unfeeling, for all intent and purposes…dead. Modern man agrees with the notion that there is no mystery here, no magical transportation of history, no miracle which invest the receiver of a gentle breeze with any kind of a change of heart. Today we continue to look at the structure of atoms, we continue to dissect them into their increasingly tiny component parts, photons, plasmas, quarks, arcs, energy...and we marvel at the fact that the laws of physics, by which all matter seems to conduct itself, are absolutely defied by these tiny pieces of energy that form our basic construction and yet are never capable of being seen by the naked eye or any mechanical lens, we simply need to have faith in the necessary conclusions of science and math. Modern man has no problem with this type of faith!

I am not a science basher nor do I want to be, Science is truly wonderful. I like to imagine myself on the top of a skyscraper in the most modern city in the world. From this viewpoint it is easy to appreciate the innovation and marvels of science and all of the interconnectivity it promotes. Millions of computers communicating in all sorts of different ways, subways, trains, roads, cars, buses, street lights, skyscrapers, public works...wastewater management, medications, vaccines, energy production and delivery, the energy grid, space exploration, phones and internet, instant communication, hospitals emergency and normal services to name a few (healthcare) in order to regulate, manage and enrich daily life. Anyone would be hard pressed to say that we would be better off without it. There are always, it seems, those who would like to return to a much more "self sufficient" time which would reject all of the advancements of technology but I think it is safe to say that the cat is already out of the bag. The solution is not in encouraging some kind of massive revolution in which governments are overthrown and many lives are lost for the sole purpose of installing someone else's values upon what is seen as a needful population. The answer is encouraging the only kind of revolution that can ever truly accomplish anything and that is the revolution of self, the encouragement of each individual to wage war within and embrace their better natures.

How in the world could or can anyone make decisions this way? There are threats all around, those who want to steal our money or our time, those who want to take advantage of our good will, those who would seek to steal even our identity, those who care about nothing except themselves. The news is hard to watch but yet we do! Embracing our better natures requires a change of focus or the acknowledgement of the value of a fresh perspective, it requires the ability to every once in a while liberate oneself from the prison of the *way things are* or *the way things have to be*. Science has expertly been going about analyzing all there is to analyze especially in relation to atoms and their component parts and very good things have come about as a result but ultimately an individual change of focus can or could bring about something much more valuable. One could stop focusing on a purely modern and therefore technological point of view which concentrates only on the physical aspects of this or that and instead focus on something like what the atoms that make up one's own body may be supporting or protecting. The current scientific climate often uses entropy (*process or cycle of constant decay followed by rebirth*) as a tool for describing the nature of things especially in relation to the creation of the universe or what is referred to as "the big bang". This concept has a number of advantages. It works well on a mathematical level in helping to explain the ever expanding universe as well as the position and rotation of the planets. It even works well on a spiritual level for those who are fearful of the end of days or the end of their own life. The primary question is always "What will happen to me?" The concept of entropy puts forth the idea of continuous rebirth in which some can find a sense of comfort for themselves as well as for the world. Taking a different point of view, Richard Gildard in a book entitled, "The Spiritual teaching of Ralph Waldo Emerson," puts forth the opposite idea, "Human Beings are designed to overcome entropy, not express it." This ancient but yet somehow fresh perspective invites one to consider the common sense idea that there is something within us all, something within each one of our atoms, that is constant. This something is the Spirit of God.

> *"In the woods we return to reason and faith. There I feel that nothing can befall me in life – no disgrace, no calamity, which nature cannot repair. Standing on the bare ground- my head bathed by the blithe air and uplifted into infinite space – all mean egotism vanishes. I am nothing, I see all; the currents of the Universal Being circulate through me; I am part or parcel of God."* Ralph Waldo Emerson, *Nature.*

Would this be a revolutionary position or stance? Maybe, but certainly one of which science would have to be skeptical. What is more apparent is our refusal to acknowledge (tendency to turn away from) the mystery and miracle of something like a breeze because we would prefer something to put our finger on, something we can put under a lens, where we can say, "Here, this is God". This need is misguided.

> *I think again about the breeze,*
> *I think again about taking in its message,*
> *I think again about how it made and makes me feel,*
> *I think again about breathing out and I do...*

The freshness of it swells my empty lungs, and I must conclude that the breeze always encourages me toward new points of view, new vistas from which to see God's presence in the world today. In order to see this presence I must be unafraid of the changing winds all around and embrace the idea that as much as I need to breathe in I also need to breathe out. *"Likewise the Spirit helps us in our weakness; for we do not know how to pray as we ought, but the Spirit himself intercedes for us with sighs too deep for words"* Romans 8: 26.

Walking forward with an open mind carries with it the challenge of not sequestering God in a particular compartment or experiment of our lives but rather in seeing and responding to His presence by reaching out to others in community.

Endnotes

1. Henri J.M. Nouwen, Reaching Out, The three movements of the spiritual life, Doubleday Publishing, 1975 p 36.
2. Gerald G May, M.D., The Dark Night of the Soul, Harper Collins Publishers, 2004, p 196
3. Gerald G May, M.D., The Dark Night of the Soul, Harper Collins Publishers, 2004, p 197
4. Gerald G May, M.D., Care of Mind, Care of Spirit, Harper Collins Publishers, 1992, P159
5. M. Craig Barnes, Reclaiming the Heidelberg Catechism, Faith Alive Christian Resources, 2012, p25
6. Ibid, p26
7. Ibid,p27
8. Gerald May, The Awakened Heart, Harper One Publishing, New York, 1991,p43
9. Ibid p43
10. Ibid
11. Pierre Teilhard de Chardin, The Human Phenomenon, Sussex Academic Press, Oregon 1999.p120, 124
12. Ibid p123
13. Kurtz, K. Ketcham, The Spirituality of Imperfection, Bantam Publishing, New York 2002 p 20, 19
14. Ibid p22

15. Gerald G May, M.D., Addiction and Grace, Love and Spirituality in the Healing of Addiction, Harper Collins Publishers, 1998, p1

16. Ibid, p,2

17. Henri J.M. Nouwen, Out of Solitude, Three Meditations on the Christian Life, Ave Maria Press, Notre Dame, 1977, p43.

18. Alcoholics Anonymous, How it Works, 3rd ed, AA World Services, New York

19. John Calvin, Institutes of Christian Religion, Hendrickson Publishing, 2014,Bk 1, 5.

20. Ibid

21. John Calvin, Institutes of Christian Religion, Hendrickson Publishing, 2014,Bk 1, 8.

22. Paul Tillich, A History of Christian Thought, Simon and Schuster, New York 1968, p8

23. Ibid p9

24. Ibid p8

25. Paul Tillich, The Courage to be, Yale University Press, 1980,p13

26. Ibid p13

27. Paul Tillich, A History of Christian Thought, Simon and Schuster, New York 1968, p7

28. Carl E Braaten, Paul Tillich and the Classical Christian Tradition, A History of Christian Thought, p,xxiv.

29. Sorren Kierkegaard, Fear and Trembling, Penguin Books, New York 1985, p78

30. Richard Rohr, Breathing Under Water, St Anthony Messenger Press, Ohio, 2011.

CPSIA information can be obtained
at www.ICGtesting.com
Printed in the USA
BVHW03*1051230818
525424BV00004B/21/P